*
G   12,754

635.9676 Gottehrer, Dean M
GO   Natural landscaping / by Dean M.
         Gottehrer. -- 1st ed. -- New York :
         Dutton, c1978.
            ix, 182 p. : ill. ; 24 cm.

            "A Sunrise book."
            Bibliography: p. 179-182.
            ISBN 0-87690-280-8

            1. Landscape gardening. 2. Wild
         flower gardening. I. Title.

SB473.G59 1978   635.9'676
                                           77-92356
                                            MARC
Library of Congress
09243   N   533389   B   © THE BAKER & TAYLOR CO.   8173

NATURAL LANDSCAPING

by Dean M. Gottehrer

A SUNRISE BOOK

E.P. Dutton   New York

To Sheila—Who both knows and understands

For information contact: E.P. Dutton, 2 Park Avenue, New York, N.Y. 10016

Library of Congress Catalog Card Number: 77-92356

ISBN: 0-87690-280-8

Published simultaneously in Canada by Clarke, Irwin & Company Limited, Toronto and Vancouver

10 9 8 7 6 5 4 3 2 1
First Edition

CONTENTS

PREFACE

The function of landscape design is more than the direct design of outdoor space arrangements. In the larger sense it is the continuous establishment of relations between man and the land, tying in those hills and valleys and broad panoramas which are beyond design, through designed elements which establish a scale relationship between each individual human and the large landscape, placing them so that individual gets a maximum experience from the relationship.

—Garrett Eckbo, *Landscape for Living*, 1950

At first glance the concept of natural landscaping might appear to be a contradiction in terms. If it's natural, then it cannot have been designed by a person. If it's landscaped by a person, then it cannot be natural. According to this viewpoint, a truly natural landscape can be found only in a wild forest, in a jungle untouched by humans, or in the wilderness. The opposite of this would be the highly structured, totally designed, formal gardens of England, France, and Italy where the plants, trees, and bushes are pruned and carved into shapes and forms that come from one's imagination, not from the wild.

Natural landscaping is somewhere between these two extremes. It avoids the apparent chaos of the wilderness as well as the structure of a formal garden.

The natural landscape designer might begin with a tract of land that has never been developed. Often crowded with large, tall trees forming a canopy of branches and leaves overhead, and thick with underbrush that makes walking difficult, this land certainly does not boast any breathtaking views, any scenery worth watching, or any beauty to contemplate.

Untamed land is the natural landscape designer's raw material in much the same way a sculptor's is a huge piece of granite. All the beauty the granite is capable of assuming is in the sculptor's mind's eye. And all the beauty the landscape is capable of exhibiting is in the designer's mind's eye.

The granite and the land are raw materials which, when lovingly sculpted and managed, become an experience of beauty for the beholder. While few people are artists and sculptors capable of great works of art, anyone can design a natural landscape that is pleasing.

The natural landscape designer works in harmony with nature by deciding where to site the house, how to structure the home's entrance, which trees to cut and which to leave, and how to create scenic views and paths, while still conserving the natural appearance of the land and the vegetation that grows upon it. The result requires little or no maintenance, since nature takes care of itself after it is encouraged to go in the designed direction.

The principles of natural landscaping, detailed in Chapter 2, are few. They can be applied in virtually any type of setting from a small urban backyard to a medium-sized suburban lot or a large rural acreage. The resulting landscapes will all appear to be different by using different trees, bushes, shrubs, plants, and ground cover. However, the underlying principles are the same no matter what size lot the home is located on, no matter whether the land is flat, hilly, or mountainous, no matter whether it is located in the forests of Maine, the plains of Illinois, the foothills of the Appalachians, or the spectacular mountain inclines above the valleys around Los Angeles.

Every site can be designed to work in harmony with nature. Every home can have natural landscaping and every result will appear to be different.

Throughout history, the architectural styles used for home design and the surrounding landscape have reflected the perceptions, concerns, culture and climate, of the people who originated and executed them.

This is still true today. The free-wheeling, leisurely lifestyle of a California family is reflected in the open, contemporary homes often spiced with a Spanish or Mexican flavor. The more formal, steady lifestyle of a crusty New Englander is reflected in his snug, warm Cape-styled home. Climate, of course, has much to do with lifestyles and strongly influences how people design their homes and relate to the landscape and environment around them.

In today's world, ecology and the environment are becoming increasingly important concerns reflected in home design and landscape. Every day, more homes are being heated by solar energy than ever before in the history of the United States. Housing design and construction also reflect the concern for increased oil, gas, and electric costs.

At the same time, landscape design has become much more informal and attuned to nature. More and more people are discovering that by planting local, natural trees, bushes, shrubs, and flowers, and stocking ponds with local fish, they are applying the lessons of ecology to their own lives and enjoying a bountiful harvest of beauty besides.

As long as the result looks natural, the landscaper can intervene as little or as much as she/he feels is necessary to sculpt and assist nature in creating a pleasureful design that will be appealing all year round, and fill the vision of the residents with the joys of seeing nature work on that plot of earth surrounding their home.

If you want to landscape your home in harmony with nature, in a way that will require little or no maintenance once the vegetation is planted and established, you can do it. You don't need professional help—unless you want it. All you will need to begin and to create your own original natural landscape design is found in the following pages.

PLAN AHEAD   **1**

Each environment has a problem to be met, and the landscaper must select in the way of plants, rocks, water, et cetera, those which fit and are in right relation to one another in the whole composition to bring out the character of the landscape in full measure. It is an understanding of the plant itself, of its real beauty, that is most essential in the art of landscaping. Without this there can be no particular feeling, no profound love, nothing to feed the deeper feelings of the human soul. There can be no feeling of love and tolerance and unselfishness.

Jens Jensen, Siftings, 1939

Traditional landscaping organizes the land around a house into certain accepted patterns. The goals of natural landscaping are different. They seek to set aside places where you can appreciate and study nature, places to watch the sun rise and set, wildflowers grow, wild animals play, trees shed their leaves, and bushes bud and bloom. A natural landscape is a place of privacy, a shelter from the day-to-day world of noise and striving, and a place where you feel comfortable, relaxed, and free to putter around with your plants. And you should be able to achieve all of this with a minimum amount of work.

Perhaps the most work comes in the beginning. Before you even lift a rake, scratch the soil, or move a single stone, you should inventory your present landscape, study the local vegetation, develop a plan of action, and decide if your plan will work. The more time and effort you devote to advance thought and planning, the less chance that you will have to rearrange your trees and bushes later on.

INVENTORY THE LANDSCAPE

The first step in developing a plan is determining what you have on your property at present. List every tree—by name if you know it.

1

Make note of every bush, shrub, and other plants. List the interesting spots in your landscape—clumps of trees, bushes, wildflowers, and perennials. As you make your lists, note any seasonal changes in the vegetation—attractive flowers, colorful leaf changes in the fall, and animal shelters in the winter.

Take your time making the inventory because it will become the base upon which you will build your plan. A year is not too long to spend—it will allow you to observe your landscape during all the seasons. A plant that appears dull and seems to contribute nothing one season suddenly may burst forth and add a splash of color in another.

Include in your inventory an inquiry into the ecology of the area. Examine your soil to determine its quality. Send samples to be tested by the nearest agricultural extension service. Or buy a soil-testing kit and do it yourself. Take note of the amount of rain and annual snowfall, the available sunlight and where it falls during the year, any pollution in the air, noise from streets or highways, and existing traffic patterns in and around your property.

While you are making your inventory, become acquainted with the local vegetation. Learn which plants are chosen by local gardeners and landscapers because they are hardy growers. Find out which plants seem to need constant attention.

For a wealth of ideas and suggestions, seek out the nearest botanical garden, arboretum, nursery, or extension service. No one has a monopoly on ideas for the natural landscape, but as long as you are going to seek inspiration, seek it from the best. These places, along with the books listed in the bibliography, will show you the variety in nature (see Chapter Thirteen). The botanical gardens and arboretums are well worth a visit. There you can see everything growing in nature and know what the plants and trees will look like once you have established them in your landscape. Since these are usually demonstration projects, you can ask the staff for help and find out what the requirements are for various trees and other plants. The staff will also assist you by suggesting local suppliers. And sometimes, when no local supplier exists, your interest may be rewarded with seeds, cuttings, or seedlings from the arboretum itself.

As you visit these places and make your inventory, remember that the natural landscape should serve the needs of all the family. Discuss with them what they like and dislike about the landscape. The more ideas you have from others, the better and more refined your plan will become. These discussions should continue as your plan is developed and put into action.

As you inventory the different elements of your landscape, make some preliminary judgments about each item and whether you wish to eliminate it or preserve it in the final design. There may be some bushes or small plants whose location you do not like and yet you hesitate to remove them. Note that. If you learn the name of each plant in your inventory it will help you make these decisions. Tree, bush, and flower identification books are available in paperback to help you with this task. After you have identified these plants, learn as much as you can about their growing patterns and their soil, moisture, and sunlight requirements. Any additional information you acquire along the way will be to your advantage.

DEVELOP A PLAN

When you have gathered all the information needed to complete your inventory, you can begin to formulate your plan. Buy some graph and tracing paper and a 50- or 100-foot tape measure. If you have a plot plan or can obtain one easily, you will be one step ahead in the process. If not, measure your property and plot it on the graph paper in scale. Locate your house and draw it in scale, and then use the tracing paper to draw the present landscape. Measure and locate all of the prominent features and groups of features from the inventory. On the remaining tracing paper, develop new landscape plans to your heart's content. Don't erase on any of the designs—take a new piece of tracing paper. Save all of the ideas you have.

As you build your design, take into account your landscape's individual needs. Do not attempt to copy a design whole cloth. That usually doesn't work because every home and its grounds present a

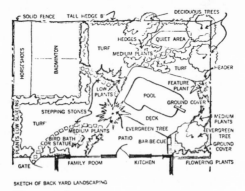

SKETCH OF BACK YARD LANDSCAPING

Figure 1-1

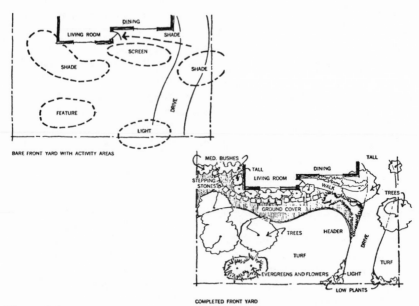

BARE FRONT YARD WITH ACTIVITY AREAS

COMPLETED FRONT YARD

Figure 1-2

unique situation. Moreover, there probably are different elements from different designs that you want to incorporate into your own plan. There may be certain effects you wish to add to your landscape, such as windbreaks, meadows, or a body of water. Consider how any new features may affect the traffic pattern as people walk through and experience your landscape.

Try to do as little as possible to create the natural landscape you want. Use restraint. Don't try to pile in every pretty native tree, wildflower, or shrub that you see. You are not trying to create your own botanical garden or arboretum. You're simply trying to do the best you can with the nature on your property. You should strive for unity and harmony, not a hodge-podge of local plants.

As you develop your plan, visualize how the vegetation will look when first planted and then when it is mature. Try to see each variation in your mind's eye, but don't be overly concerned if you can't. What is important is that you have a clear concept of what you are attempting to do. The concept may change as the plan evolves, and you may see things you never noticed before, but throughout your concept should be clear in your mind.

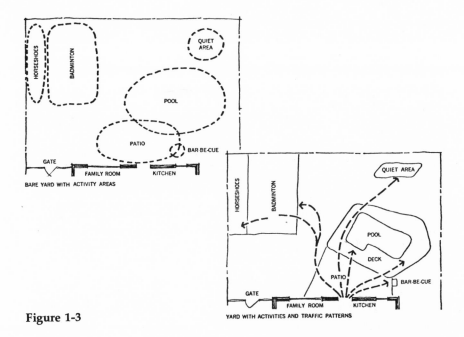

Figure 1-3

Before you decide on the plan you want to implement, stake it out. If you are a model builder, you might try to construct a scale model. Most people, however, will be more comfortable staking their design out directly on their land. From the drawing you have made, measure everything you want to add and then place the stakes at the appropriate places. You can use twine or rope to mark the boundaries of large ground cover beds or wildflower beds. Bricks or rocks can be used to mark the boundaries of ponds or pools.

Once you have staked everything out, move around in the design you have created. See if there is something you want to remove. You may think of something to add. Have you inadvertently blocked a pretty view? Have you crowded too many plants into too small an area? Make any necessary modifications. Perhaps you will need to re-stake everything a second time if the changes are substantial.

As you proceed through this planning process, realize that you are not going to create the perfect plan. What you are attempting to do is to place the proper plant in the proper place. Nature spent a great deal of time placing plants in the best locales for them to grow, so you should not feel rushed. (After all, it's substantially easier to move trees, plants, bushes, and shrubs around on paper than it is to move them around in your landscape.) Spend as much time as you wish in developing your design. Play with it, change it, putter around with it, show it to neighbors and friends and ask for their comments, discuss it with the family. What you are attempting to do is to build and perfect a design that you can be happy with. You will finally reach a point when you feel it is as close to perfection as you can make it. Then it is time to put aside the tracing paper.

If you are not making extensive changes in your landscape, you may be able to put the plan into action in less than a year. If you have a great number of changes you wish to make, take your time and make the changes slowly.

Beginning with bare earth, first add the shade trees, then a meadow or lawn, followed by shrubs or bushes and finally other plants. You may then want to consider a pool, or a rock garden, or a play area. You can use this order also for making changes on an already established property.

If you follow the suggestions and principles described later in the book, you will find that you can create a landscape around your home that is pleasing to look at, easy to care for, and worth the amount of time and thought that went into developing it. Most of all, you will be proud to have created a landscape design where nature's strongest, hardiest, and attractive aspects are encouraged, demonstrated, and passed along to the next generation.

THEORY AND 2
CONCEPTS OF
NATURAL
LANDSCAPING

Parks and gardens of curves are always new, always revealing new thoughts and new interests in life. Straight lines are copies from the architect and do not belong to the landscaper. They have nothing to do with nature, of which landscaping is a part and out of which the art has grown. Landscaping must follow the lines of the free-growing tree with its thousands of curves. One might hope that in developing a beautiful outlook on life the youth of our country would learn the life of a tree and its tremendous importance.

Jens Jensen, *Siftings*, 1939

Landscape designs for the home traditionally have been divided into two basic categories — formal and naturalistic. Formal designs are composed of straight lines, squares, rectangles, circles, and other geometric shapes arranged in perfect symmetry around a central point. Naturalistic designs are composed of great flowing lines and irregular shapes and forms, often arranged in massive blocks, and are considered to be less artificial and more romantic than formal designs.

At their best, both styles provide pleasing and functional ways in which to organize the home grounds and make them not merely livable but enjoyable as well. Neither style, however, can truly be described as natural. The flowing curves and irregular shapes of the naturalistic designs come closer to nature than do the geometry of the formal designs. However, it is usually obvious in a naturalistic design that humans placed the plants, trees, bushes, and other elements— that the design had a human plan. There is nothing wrong with a human plan, but it is much easier and in the end more pleasing to follow nature's lead.

7

Fig. 2-1 *Natural landscape by Jens Jensen (Courtesy of Leonard K. Eaton and University of Michigan, College of Architecture Library)*

WORKING WITH NATURE

Natural landscaping begins with the designs of nature, not of humans, and so the first principle is to work with nature, not against it. Before you design your plan, look at what already exists on your grounds. Follow the course of action described in Chapter One. See what the different seasons bring. Discover what nature has already provided.

Leaving nature alone.   Sometimes the best way to work with nature is to leave it alone—to not touch anything at all. What will happen if you do nothing on your grounds for one year, five years, fifty years? Do you know? If not, you may make mistakes that will cost time, effort, and perhaps money to correct. You may have just become the proud owner of a newly built tract development house on a bulldozed lot or perhaps the heir to acreage that has been in the family for generations. Before you do anything, you should know what will happen to your land if you leave it alone and let nature run its course.

In the Northeast much farmland has been abandoned. So many crops were grown that the diminished value of the land made it difficult for farmers to continue farming, and they sold out to developers. Abandoned farmland is a good example of how nature passes through a cycle. This natural cycle has been studied by ecologists and environmentalists. In the first years following abandonment, fields bring forth annual weeds such as ragweed, pigweed, beggarweed, gooseweed, purslane, and foxtail grass. These are tall rangy weeds that start each year from seed. During the next stage, a few years later, the grasses, perennial herbs, and some of the larger forbs such as daisies, goldenrods, asters, and eupatoriums, begin to dominate. The forbs tend to kill off the grasses because they are larger and more aggressive.

As more years pass, shrubs and sun-loving trees begin to emerge. These include red cedar, juniper, cherry, birch, aspen, and hawthorn—the kinds depend on what was present before the field was cultivated as well as on soil, moisture, and other environmental factors.

Ten to twenty years after abandonment, the sun-loving trees take over the field—it becomes a treeland. Forty years after being abandoned, the field begins to show shade-loving seedlings under the protection of their sun-loving companions. Within 100 years the shade-loving trees will have taken over the forest and provided a home for their seedlings underneath.

This is a vastly simplified version of what can be a very complex process. Variations on the theme depend on: what was present before the field was cultivated (were the trees that were cut down killed and roots taken out—if not they may grow again); whether there was any interference along the way from fire, flood, pasturing, or mowing (if so, this may stunt the growth of some elements of the forest and prevent the growth of others); and whether much of the succeeding vegetation was present when the field was abandoned (some tree seedlings, for example, may have been present when the annual weeds first made their appearance). This simplified description of the process will help you understand that the nature of vegetation on your land is not static. It will change if you leave it alone.

Once you have figured out what stage of development your property is in, you can work with it, encourage the plants and trees you wish to see emerge, discourage others you wish to eliminate, and develop a landscape based on natural processes rather than one structured entirely by human design and influence.

You can create a meadow by keeping an area in grasslands. Watch carefully for the emergence of shrubs and tree seedlings. If you see these unwanted plants beginning to invade, you can remove them (using methods detailed later) and preserve your meadow. (You may choose to allow part of your land to become a forest by not removing the tree seedlings.)

When you do decide to make changes in nature, remember that it's hard to make just one change and leave it at that. Making a change in nature is like dropping a rock into a pond. No matter how hard you try, there are always ripples that disturb the water's surface. When you are making plans for a change, list the possible benefits and damages. See if the damage is avoidable. Observe what others value as beauty even though you may not. Keep all of your senses open to the beauty of your surrounding landscape and you will be sure to preserve and protect it.

LOW MAINTENANCE PLANTS

The amount of maintenance your landscape needs is determined by the types of plants, trees, and bushes you allow to prosper or choose to add. One of the benefits of a natural landscape is that it needs little or no maintenance. Nature does all the work for you. A plant that is not native to the local environment requires more maintenance. Such plants usually need frequent watering, fertilizing, staking, pruning, or spraying to control disease. They may be unable to survive freezing winters, dry spells, excessive heat, or poor drainage.

Native plants almost always require less maintenance, and some plants are known for their ability to thrive on low or no maintenance at all. Although some of the plants listed here are not natives, they are available from nurseries and you may find them already growing on established landscapes. You should know what they are and value their ability to prosper with little or no attention.

Trees and Shrubs

The U.S. Department of Agriculture has developed a list of 26 minimum-care flowering shrubs, vines, and trees. These are noted with the coldest zone in which the plant is hardy. The zones are keyed to the plant hardiness map on page 22. These plants should be placed in an area where they can grow large over time and not crowd each other. The plants are listed in order of flowering sequence beginning in the spring.

Plant	Zone	Colors
Hamamelis species (Witch-hazel)	2	Yellow
Cornus mas (Cornelian cherry)	3	Yellow
Forsythia species (Forsythia)	2	Yellow
Pieris japonica (Japanese andromeda)	4	Pink-to-red, white
Amelanchier canadensis (Serviceberry)	3	White
Chaenomeles japonica (Japanese quince)	3	Red, orange
Magnolia soulangeana (Saucer magnolia)	2	Pink and white
Spiraea vanhouttei (Bridal wreath)	3	White
Spiraea thunbergi (Japanese spirea)	3	White
Cercis canadensis (American redbud)	3	Purplish-pink, white
Cornus florida (Flowering dogwood)	4	White and pink
Deutzia grandiflora (Deutzia)	4	White
Kerria japonica (Kerria)	3	Yellow
Syringa vulgaris (Common lilac)	2	Lilac, white
Kolkwitzia amabilis (Beauty-bush)	3	Pink
Weigela florida (Weigela)	3	White, rose, pink
Kalmia latifolia (Mountain laurel)	3	Pink and white
Hydrangea arborescens (Hills-of-snow)	3	Creamy white
Calluna vulgaris (Heather)	4	White, pink, and red
Abelia grandiflora (Glossy abelia)	4	Pink
Buddleia davidi (Butterfly-bush)	4	White, pink, red, or purple
Caryopteris incana (Blue spirea)	5	Misty-blue
Hibiscus syriacus (Althea, Rose-of-Sharon)	3	White and blue
Lagerstroemia indica (Crape myrtle)	5	Pink to red
Sophora japonica (Japanese pagoda tree)	3	Blue-violet
Vitex agnus-castus (Chaste tree)	5	Lilac or pale violet

A pruning every year or every other year will keep these shrubs and trees within the space allotted. Left alone, they will continue to grow and eventually become very large.

Bulbs and Perennials

The Department of Agriculture has also developed a list of 25 minimum-care flowering herbaceous perennials and bulbs. These plants can be placed underneath the flowering trees and shrubs and do not require frequent lifting and division or protection from pests and disease. The zones are keyed to the plant hardiness map on p. 22. They flower in the following sequence from late winter to fall.

Plant	Zone	Colors
Helleborus niger (Christmas rose)	3	White with rose
Galanthus species (Snowdrop)	3	White
Crocus vernus (Crocus)	4	Lilac or white
Muscari species (Grape-hyacinth)	4	Blue or violet
Narcissus species (Daffodil)	4	White and yellow
Leucojum aestivum (Snowflake)	4	White with green tips
Scilla hispanica (Spanish bluebell)	4	Blue-to-rose-purple
Convallaria majalis (Lily-of-the-valley)	2–3	Yellow, light pink
Dicentra spectabilis (Bleeding-heart)	2–3	Pink, white
Dicentra cucullaria (Dutchman's-breeches)	3	White-to-pink
Aquilegia hybrids (Columbine)	2–3	Many colors
Paeonia species (Peony)	3	Light pink-to-deep red or white
Lilium candidum (Madonna lily)	4	White
Astilbe species (False goat's beard)	5	White, pink, red, or purple
Heuchera sanguinea hybrids (Coral bells)	3	Red-to-pink, white
Iris species (Bearded and beardless iris)	3	Purple, red, or brown
Primula hybrids (Primrose)	2–3	Variety of colors
Oenothera species (Evening primrose)	3	Generally yellow
Lilium regale (Regal lily)	3	White-to-rose-purple
Hemerocallis species (Daylilies)	2–3	Orange, yellow, or red
Canna (Canna)	7	Yellow, pink-to-red
Sedum species (Stonecrop)	3	White, yellow, pink, red-to-purple

Plant	Zone	Colors
Eupatorium collestinum (Bluemist-flower)	3	White, purple
Lycoris squamigera (Lycoris)	5	Lilac-rose
Colchicum autumnale (Autumn crocus)	4	Rose-purple, white

The Natural Lawn. The home landscaper often spends an inordinate amount of time, effort, and money to create a lush, verdant, carpet of a lawn that will be the envy of neighbors for miles around. The natural landscaper, instead of investing all that energy and expense, sits back and watches the grass grow higher and higher. Suddenly instead of a lawn you have—a meadow.

Of course you don't have to give up your lawn completely. You may want to keep a small area for picnics and barbecues, for croquet and other lawn games, or perhaps for a putting green.

Not only have you reduced the amount of time needed to mow your lawn, but you have also eliminated the need for fertilizing and

Fig. 2-2 *The sloping thicket selected for naturalistic landscaping on the Mattheis Tract of the Connecticut Arboretum. The first of a sequence of four views. Sumac and wild black cherry with mixed grasses in foreground. Note the red cedar and gray birch (Photo 1953). (Courtesy Connecticut Arboretum)*

Fig. 2-3 *The naturalistically landscaped demonstration area five years after its establishment. The more attractive columnar red cedar and gray birch have been accented in a relatively open matrix of grass and scattered shrubs. The two planted white pines in the foreground were subsequently removed (Photo 1958). From Connecticut Arboretum Bulletin No. 21 (1975) Connecticut College, New London, Conn. 06320. (Courtesy Connecticut Arboretum)*

watering and worrying about crabgrass and dandelions, edges that need trimming, and so on.

If your home sits squarely in the middle of a development on a very small lot, you must consider the impact on your neighbors when you let the lawn become a meadow. The easiest way to lessen their ire (that is, if they don't all immediately see the wisdom of your laziness) is to plant trees and bushes around the perimeter of your property. This will provide privacy and will ward off complaints that you are creating an eyesore. From an uneducated view it may be so, but your neighbors will soon see that you have perceived the beauty inherent in natural landscaping. If you are unable to bring yourself to grow a meadow, consider a ground cover which provides an alternative to a lawn and requires little or no maintenance. Ground covers are discussed in Chapter Five.

ECOLOGICAL AND ENVIRONMENTAL IMPACT

Natural landscaping is ecologically and environmentally sound. In traditional landscaping the lawn, for example, must be mowed regularly. Today's homeowner would not be without a power mower—the bigger the lawn, the bigger the mower. Small mowers use an estimated five gallons of gasoline per year, large riding mowers, 25 gallons a year. These gallons mount up when computed nationally. What is perhaps just as important is that by using a power mower the homeowner reduces or eliminates the exercise he or she would get from using a hand mower.

Fertilizer is required to keep the lawn in good shape and growing to its full capacity. (How ironic it is that we fertilize to stimulate good growth and then mow to keep the lawn from growing too tall.) In the United States every year we use as much fertilizer on our lawns as is used in India each year for food production. And so while millions of people around the world are suffering the effects of food shortages, much of which can be traced to a shortage of fertilizer for food production (one pound of fertilizer will produce ten pounds of food), we are wasting it on our lawns. Although this may be reminiscent of when mother admonished us to clean our plate because people were starving in China, the fertilizer shortage was serious enough in recent years to compel 38 Senators to ask the President to recommend a reduction in fertilizer use on lawns to help underdeveloped countries.

Nature reuses its resources, while man tends to squander them. The leaves and grass clippings our traditional landscaper tosses into plastic bags made from nonrenewable petroleum resources are meant to feed the soil. When in autumn the leaves turn color and fall to the forest floor, microorganisms break down the leaves and the remaining chemicals then fertilize the plants and trees to create new growth. This efficient ecosystem renews and refreshes itself until man's ego system interferes.

Natural landscaping encourages ecologically and environmentally sound practices because it stimulates the landscaper to examine the natural environment, to discern the natural processes, and to work within them.

VEGETATION MANAGEMENT

At the heart of natural landscaping is the management of the vegetation surrounding your home. If you have an ample supply of vegeta-

Fig. 2-4 *The naturalistically landscaped demonstration area ten years after establishment. Flowering dogwood has been highlighted. The red cedar to the right is the same one visible in the 1953 photograph. A flowering highbush blueberry is the lighter shrub in front of the cedar. Little bluestem grassland dominates in the foreground (Photo Spring, 1964). (Courtesy Connecticut Arboretum)*

tion already provided by nature, there may be trees, bushes, and other plants you wish to be rid of for one reason or another. The tree may be blocking a beautiful view of the other side of a valley. Poison ivy may be profuse and must be eliminated. You may wish to restrict the growth of certain types of vegetation to stimulate other types, using your knowledge of the developmental cycle of your land's vegetation.

Removal of unwanted elements in your landscape can be accomplished in a variety of ways. Much can be done purely with muscle power. You can cut down a tree, pull out its roots, and be rid of it—until perhaps a piece of root you missed begins to send forth another sprout. You can ring a tree with an ax and peel off the bark, which will effectively kill it. Poison ivy, however, is almost impossible to remove in this way. If you try to pull it out, you risk a bad case of poison ivy.

Fig. 2-5 *The naturalistically landscaped area after nearly 15 years of management. The aspect is still relatively open. Notice the increased development of the red cedar and gray birch visible in the 1953 photograph. Grasses and goldenrod are in the foreground; low clonal huckleberry and tall highbush blueberry; beyond, cedars and birches. Currently the area appears the same and requires little maintenance (Photo 1967). (Courtesy Connecticut Arboretum)*

Herbicides. No matter what you want to remove from your landscape, you will eventually face the question of whether or not to use herbicides. The answer is not clear cut. Many herbicides are dangerous to humans and animals and their use has been restricted or prohibited by law. Herbicides were used in Vietnam to kill all vegetation; it was there that scientists discovered that this type of defoliation was harmful to both land and people, and yet there are natural landscapers who would not do without herbicides, prudently selected and applied to control elements in their natural landscape design that would be difficult or impossible to control otherwise. Warren Kenfield, in *The Wild Gardener in The Wild Landscape*, claims that it is impossible to do what he calls naturalistic landscaping without herbicides. He says he tried it in the 1920's, before the development of modern herbicides, and the amount of work required with pickax and shovel was simply too great.

Fig. 2-6 *Balanced symmetry is achieved by placing exactly the same plant on either side of the center. (Photo by Dean M. Gottehrer)*

Kenfield, who used herbicides such as 2,4,5–T (the defoliant used in Vietnam), compares the danger of using herbicides with that of caffeine in coffee, salt on lunch, an alcoholic drink before dinner, and a barbiturate-induced slumber. Kenfield, although perhaps overstating the dangers of all of these, certainly was understating the dangers of the herbicides he was using.

This does not mean that you must eliminate all use of herbicides. Work at the Connecticut Arboretum in New London, Connecticut, by Drs. William A. Niering and Richard H. Goodwin, has indicated that some compounds, such as ammate, are safe to use on the home grounds if applied under proper conditions with discrimination and caution in areas where there is little danger to humans or animals. Ammonium sulfamate (ammate) is a water-soluble crystal that Dr. Goodwin recommends because it is biodegradable. As with some other herbicides, ammate is not selective in what it kills. It will kill both grasses and broad-leaved plants and when its crystals are placed in cut trunks and stumps it can be used to kill trees as well.

Fig. 2-7 *The fountain in the center and the statue at the end of the path are accents in this landscape. (Photo by Dean M. Gottehrer)*

It pays to remember that the use of herbicides, as well as pesticides, is regulated by federal law. The penalties for misusing herbicides apply to the homeowner as well as the commercial user. *All herbicides must be used in accordance with label instructions.* This means that every time you use a herbicide, you should be certain that the product is labeled as being safe and effective for the use you wish to make of it, that it will not be used on vegetation that isn't listed on the label, that it will control or kill only the type of vegetation you wish to remove and that any restrictions placed upon the product for home use will be followed.

If you decide to apply herbicides, a few precautions will help you protect yourself. Be sure you are completely clothed—no bare arms or legs. Keep children and pets away from the area where you are mixing and applying the herbicides. Choose a well-ventilated area in which to prepare the herbicide. Keep your hands away from your mouth when you are applying the mixtures—you should not eat, drink, or smoke at the same time. Keep chemicals from coming in contact with your skin—wash thoroughly after any spill on your skin and immediately after finishing any application. Wash your clothes before wearing them again and wear boots to protect your shoes. Even biodegradable herbicides can be dangerous and toxic if handled incorrectly.

You must be careful how you apply the herbicides. A mistake could eliminate a desired element from your landscape. Don't think that if a little bit is good, a lot will be much better—it won't. Always apply herbicides at the recommended rate, at the recommended time, and under the recommended conditions. It is easy to come back a second time to apply more if it is really needed, but you can't take back an overdose. Watch where you apply the herbicide—if there is a breeze, the herbicide could be carried a short distance and destroy a prized plant. If you are using a nonselective herbicide, and are applying it to roots, take care that you are not on a slope above a desired plant—the herbicide may leach down the slope and kill the plant. Once you have used herbicide in a sprayer or other container, don't use it for anything but herbicides. There is no effective way to completely remove all herbicide residues. Once you have finished, dispose of all herbicide containers in a safe manner. Rinse each container three times and get rid of the rinse water by applying it with your sprayer to plants you wish to eliminate. If you have a trash pickup, wrap each individual container in a number of layers of newspaper and tie it up securely. If you don't have trash pickup, bury the container at least a foot and a half deep where it will not contaminate the water and in an area away from any plants. Never burn containers—the resulting vapor can be dangerous. Do not pour any leftover herbicides down any drain—septic tank or sewer. They can cause problems in either place.

Exercise caution in storing herbicides. Keep them under lock and key away from children, food, and medical supplies. Store them in the original container and preserve the label. Try to keep only what you need, as you need it.

Weeds.   In examining local vegetation, keep an unbiased eye. Before removing what you think is a weed, judge whether or not it is performing a valuable function. Some weeds are friends in disguise. Ralph Waldo Emerson described a weed as "a plant whose virtues have not yet been discovered." Plants such as ragweed, annual goldenrod, nightshade, sow thistle, lamb's quarter, ground cherry, wild lettuce, and sunflowers are good soil improvers when allowed to grow in moderation. Dandelion, nettle, and thistle are high in protein. Even poison ivy produces berries of value to native wildlife and serves as a ground cover to prevent invasions of trees. Beneficial weeds hold the soil in place, break it up, and, with their deep root systems, bring minerals and other nutrients to the surface.

Adding native plants.   Herbicides help you to remove plants. Knowing the vegetation development cycle helps you to decide what plants to keep. But should you add to and embellish upon what is already present in your landscape? At one extreme are those who contend that if it isn't there, it shouldn't be there. At the other extreme are those who would rip everything out and put in all new plants. Most of us are probably somewhere in the middle and few of us can resist the impulse to add a little touch here and there. The natural land-scaper will try to limit his or her choices to native plants or nursery-bred plants that are known to thrive locally. Obviously, no gardener in New England would plant an avocado outdoors, and no Floridian would expect a sugar maple to thrive in South Florida's sandy soil. Yet gardeners in both locales and elsewhere are often tempted to try their hand at borderline cases where the chances for success might be slim but the rewards pleasureful.

The natural landscaper is not tempted. He or she chooses plants that have known characteristics, that prove successful in the growing environment, and that require little and return much. The natural landscaper studies any additions to the landscape carefully. Whether the contemplated addition is native to the local environment or not, it is known to grow there easily and provide the qualities the natural landscaper desires from his or her design.

Once you have decided to add to your landscape, what should you add? Naturalistic landscaper Warren Kenfield recommends using bulbs to enhance a grasslands area. He says that there is a certain competition between plants for the necessities of life and that broad-casting seed accomplishes little beyond feeding the birds and field mice. Bulbs, however, bring with them the sustenance needed for the plant to survive for a year and don't compete as much as seeds do to establish a place in the plant community and thrive there.

Dr. Richard H. Goodwin suggests adding a few lilies to enhance meadowland where lawn once reigned supreme.

In the following chapters, you will learn how to determine what to add and where, and what the impact of these decisions will be on your landscape and its design.

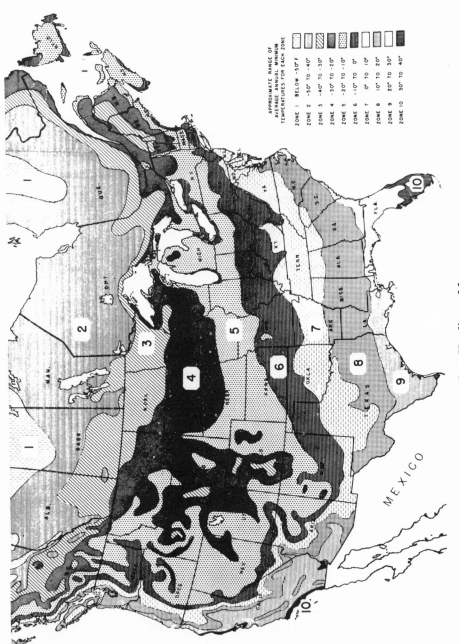

Plant Hardiness Map

PRINCIPLES OF NATURAL LANDSCAPING

Nature provides the raw materials for the landscaper to sculpt into a design that appears natural and presents a pleasing and beautiful experience. The variety nature presents to the landscaper will, if preserved, contribute to the area's stability. For example, when you have many different kinds of native plants, a disease that infects one will not kill the others.

Within the diversity nature provides, the landscaper must apply a knowledge of design in selecting vegetation to eliminate or add. As with all sets of principles, they are not to be strictly followed, but used rather as general guidelines.

Unity.   Does the landscape look as though it was thrown together in a hodge-podge chaotic way? If it does, then you will have to draw up a plan around which it can be unified. Color, texture, height, form, growth habits, lines, and perspectives can all be used to unify a landscape design. As with any work of art, the eye must be attracted to areas where you wish to focus attention. Natural landscaping allows for greater flexibility because so much of the art comes from nature and does not follow strict geometrical or formal design patterns. A little controlled chaos is permissible.

Balance.   In traditional and formal landscape design, balance is often the principle most observed. Simply stated, it means that everything on both sides of a given focal point has equal weight. With symmetrical balance, as the eye moves away from the central focal point everything is exactly the same on both sides. On either side of a walkway, for example, you may find an evergreen bush, then some tulips, then daffodils, a forsythia, more bulbs, and perhaps a maple tree. One side of the walkway is a mirror reproduction of the other. With asymmetrical balance, the exact reproduction of all elements is replaced with a more general sensation of equal weight. Tulips may balance daffodils, while different types of bushes of the same general size and shape balance each other.

Balance in the natural landscape is always asymmetrical and a question of dominance. If one side of the landscape towers above the other, there is no balance. When balance exists, there is a feeling of security and stability.

Accent.   As the eye moves over a landscape, certain points attract attention. In the formal landscape, the patterns of walkways, fountains, statues, intricately sculptured hedges, and different lines and perspectives draw attention. In the natural landscape, these focal points may be a pond or pool, a grove of trees, a clump of wildflowers in a meadow, or a shelter for animals. By drawing attention to these focal points, the natural landscaper prevents monotony of design.

Accents can be achieved by contrasts in color, texture, line, shape, height, or rhythm. A landscape where all of these elements are unified would be very boring. Varying these design factors helps the natural landscaper draw the eye to points of interest and structure the experience of the landscape to produce a sensation of beauty and enjoyment.

Size.   The correct size of trees and bushes placed correctly is the most important factor in creating a sense of proportion in the natural landscape. A postage-stamp backyard is not the place to plant a Colorado fir tree, which may grow to be 200 feet tall. Choose vegetation that will fill the space given over to it as it grows and will not require constant pruning to keep it within the available space.

Repetition.   Repetition is most often used in formal landscape design. A long straight driveway benefits from a border of stately columns of a single type of tree. Repetition does have its applications in natural landscaping and should not be overlooked. A repeated planting of wildflowers such as Jack-in-the-pulpit, for example, can function as an echo of what has passed or as a harbinger of what is yet to come. Repetition should be used sparingly in natural landscaping since it is not found frequently in nature.

Pace and order.   Look at any good representational painting. Notice that your eyes pass over it and are attracted to the painting's focal points in a certain pace and in a certain order. The same is true with a landscape. Properly designed, your eye will pass over the landscape in the order and at the rate at which the designer has structured the experience. In a good landscape design, the eye does not move randomly, flitting from one point to another. Determine if you want people to pause and look more closely at an interesting bed of wildflowers after they visit the pond. Or do you want them to pass rapidly by an area of maple trees planted with pachysandra underneath.

As you design your landscape, imagine how you want people to move through it, what you want them to look at, in what order, and how rapidly.

Texture, form, light, and color. These are not, properly speaking, principles as much as design elements to be used to execute your natural landscape design. Skillfully employed, they can create a unified, balanced, well-accented, properly proportioned landscape that needs little repetition, but takes the viewer through it in the proper pace and order. The different textures of leaves, bark, and ground covers, the different forms of flowers on bushes, trees, and perennials, and the various colors of leaves on trees, bushes, and flowering plants, when combined with the interplay of light and shadow, all help create a more varied and interesting natural landscape.

It should be obvious by now that the most important ingredient in any natural landscape design is thought. If you take your time, closely examine what you have presently in your landscape, and carefully contemplate what changes you are going to make, you will be able to devise a natural plan that requires little effort to execute and maintain and will provide pleasure for you, your family, and your friends for many years to come.

TREES 3

Trees are much like human beings and enjoy each other's company. Only a few love to be alone. Some trees like to be placed in a small group, and with their branches interlaced they give an expression of friendship. Trees that like to stand out alone or in small groups become landmarks of their surroundings. There are trees that belong to low grounds and those that have adapted themselves to highlands. They always thrive best amid the conditions they have chosen for themselves through many years of selection and elimination. They tell us that they love to grow here, and only here will they speak in their fullest measure.

Jens Jensen, Siftings, 1939

No other single element in your natural landscape affects the environment as much as trees. Lawns, flowers, bushes and shrubs, wild animals, and rock gardens are all important aesthetic factors in the design of a natural landscape. Trees, however, can control the environment as well as please the eye.

Temperature control. Take a stroll in a forest on a hot summer day and notice the difference in temperature under the trees and in the full sun. Ninety percent of the solar energy reaching a tree is absorbed by the tree's upper foliage. These leaves function much like a radiator and lower the temperature at the forest floor. The air under a tent covering the same ground area would be much warmer. The tree has five to seven times more surface on its leaves than the tent with which to absorb the sun's heat.

The temperature under a tree is also affected by a process called transpiration. Trees draw moisture from the soil up the tree stem to the leaves where it evaporates. A birch tree, for example, may transpire as much as 700 to 900 gallons of water on a hot summer day. In an area of well-watered vegetation, mostly trees, the air temperature

Fig. 3-1 *Fall foliage enhances the value of attractive trees in the natural landscape (Photo by Dean M. Gottehrer)*

will be reduced by transpiration by approximately 7°F. In the same manner, trees act as a blanket at night, keeping the ground under the tree warmer than in the surrounding area. The frost-free period is also longer under a tree than in the open.

A single large tree in an urban area can have the cooling effect of five average room-sized air conditioners running about 20 hours a day. However, this amount of transpirational cooling can take place only when there is an adequate water supply for the tree to draw upon. A tree that casts its shade on the west wall and roof of a house can reduce the interior temperature of the home between 20° and 40°F. The top three shade producers in the country are elm, maple, and oak.

The greatest reduction of the cost of home heating in the winter is gained by planting conifer trees on the two or three sides from which the prevailing winds come. These trees should be placed close to the house, but not so close as to cast a shadow since you also want to take advantage of the sun's heating rays. In the Plains states a windbreak of three rows of evergreens and three rows of deciduous trees at a distance of 100 to 150 feet from the house provides optimum protection. To take advantage of the air-conditioning effect of shade and transpiration in the summer, plant rows of deciduous trees so that they will cast shadows on the west and south walls of your home. Since deciduous trees shed their leaves in the winter, you can place them closer to the house than you can evergreens.

Tree barriers.   Trees are also used to create barriers to the wind. In the Great Plains of the Midwest, many farm houses are surrounded on several sides by trees to prevent the wind from cooling the house in winter. The importance of such a windbreak is evident from its impact on fuel consumption. It takes twice the amount of fuel to heat a house at 32°F with a12-mile-per-hour wind as it does to heat the same house at the same temperature with only a 3-mile-per-hour wind. Or to put it another way, the same amount of fuel will heat a house at 32°F with a 12-mile-per-hour wind or at 0°F with a 3-mile-per-hour wind. A double row of maple trees at least 40 feet tall will reduce a wind blowing at them perpendicularly by 50 percent on the downwind side. The effect tapers as the wind changes from a 90° angle to the trees.

Trees can also be used for a sound barrier, for example, between your home and a nearby road or highway. The tree's leaves act as baffles and disperse the sound before it reaches your ears. Intensely loud areas will require more trees and may require a mixture of deciduous and coniferous trees.

A windbreak or sound barrier of trees will also reduce snow drifting; by shading the snow on the ground, it prevents it from melting too rapidly and eroding land as it runs off. Trees also prevent erosion by holding the soil with their roots; they also hold water and snow in their leaves so that moisture does not reach the ground as quickly as when there are no trees. A tree will intercept between 15 and 20 percent of a rainfall and even more of snowfall as long as there is no more than a light wind. Dust downwind from a tree barrier can be reduced by as much as 75 percent.

The forest canopy.   In the forest trees tend to create a canopy high above ground. This canopy allows only certain kinds of shrubs and other vegetation to grow. These plants do not grow in the same manner under the forest canopy as they would in the open. If you cut just one tree, you influence virtually every other element in the forest— air, water, soil, other trees, plants, animals, and so on. However, it is often necessary to open up the canopy.

Fig. 3-2 *If you can leave the dead tree stump, it will attract animal and vegetable life that will thrive on its remains. (Photo by Dean M. Gottehrer)*

To partially clear a forest for seasonal use in the summer, clear out the underbrush and prune branches so that they will not hurt anyone. If there are short trees present, make small east-to-west clearings in such a manner as to leave tall trees on the south side of the clearing to shade your summer activities. For winter activities north-to-south clearings are made, keeping evergreens on the north and west sides to protect against the winds and deciduous trees on the south side to let the sun shine through in winter.

To partially open the canopy it is best to cut only one tree. This allows more light to come to the forest floor, stimulating new growth and increasing the health of the remaining trees by reducing the competition. Trees that grow too close together tend to do poorly because they don't get enough light, air, and water.

If you are going to clear away underbrush, don't clear it all because that will slowly kill the forest. Clearing out all of the underbrush removes seedlings that otherwise would eventually become adult trees replacing those that die.

Consider leaving dead trees standing. These trees may support wildlife in the forest (see Chapter Nine). You should cut them down only when they have a disease or would otherwise endanger other trees, the house, or people using a nearby path through the forest. Trees that you do cut down can be used as fireplace fuel.

TREE INVENTORY

The first step toward improving the trees in your landscape is to inventory the kinds of trees presently growing on your grounds. List each tree individually, determine its shape, its stage of growth (Is it full grown?), its root system (Do the roots tend to be on the surface or deeper down?), its condition of health (Is it vigorous and growing or straggly, weak, and perhaps dying?), whether it is deciduous or coniferous, and whether or not the tree bears flowers and fruit.

As you inventory each tree, attempt to assess its contribution to your landscape. Does it provide needed shade in the summer or act as a windbreak in the winter? Does it add aesthetically to the landscape, or does it block a beautiful view? Does it cause increased maintenance, either because it drops fruit and nuts or excessive amounts of leaves on the lawn interfering with mowing, or because it is prone to insect and disease damage calling for constant attention? If the tree is in less than good health, can it be brought back to good health by a professional arborist or tree surgeon? Is the tree worth saving? As you inventory the trees, you are gathering information to help you decide whether the tree should remain, be taken down, or replaced. Do not rush to a decision. The trees have been on your ground for a long time and another year or two before you decide won't hurt.

If you are preparing to build a home, you want to be sure you evaluate the trees present on your grounds *before construction begins* and decide which ones to save and which ones to remove. Ask yourself these questions about each tree: Will a tree in this location provide shade where I want it? Will it reduce or eliminate sunlight where I need it for winter warmth and for my lawn and garden? Will the tree protect my home from winter winds or prevent the circulation of summer breezes? Will it hide an unpleasant view or block out a desirable one? Will the roots crack a sidewalk or driveway? Do the roots grow close to the surface (as do those of maple, linden, dogwood, and most conifers), and cause problems in growing my lawn and some ornamental shrubs? Will the tree, because of its age or species, have difficulty adapting to changes caused by construction? Old and larger trees generally do not adapt to change as well as younger and smaller trees of the same species. Elm, poplar, willow, plane tree, and locust adapt well to change. Beeches, birches, hickories, tulip trees, some oaks, and most conifers and maples are less adaptable.

During construction trees must be protected from three hazards—equipment and supplies, raising or lowering the surrounding soil grade, and excavations for sewer and water lines. Trees can be protected from construction equipment by building a simple fence or barrier around the tree. Changes in grade or excavations may justify the expense of professional assistance from a landscape architect, arborist, nurseryman, forester, or county agricultural agent. The last person to trust is a construction worker who probably knows about as much concerning tree protection techniques as does the average home owner.

Once you have inventoried your trees and made your decisions, you can begin to remove the ones that detract from the natural environment and add others that will strengthen it.

TREE REMOVAL

The method you use to kill a tree will depend on whether or not you wish to leave the tree standing once it is dead. Diseased trees and those you are removing to open up the canopy will obviously have to come down. Trees you are killing in order to remove some of the competition can be left standing. It is often necessary, after taking a tree down, to remove the stump to prevent further new growth. Stumps can be pulled out, burned, dynamited, or killed by an herbicide such as ammate. Ammate crystals can be placed directly on the stump to kill it. If there is no need to remove the stump, consider using it to create a rest spot. If you take the tree down yourself, or if you have a professional do it for you, be sure the cuts are made in such a way as to leave the bottom half of the stump at a convenient level for sitting and the top half long enough to provide back support. You may wish to add a plank to increase the seating area.

If you wish to kill the tree but leave it standing, you can girdle it by cutting through the outer and inner bark, leaving at least an inch or more of bare wood showing all around the tree trunk. This can be

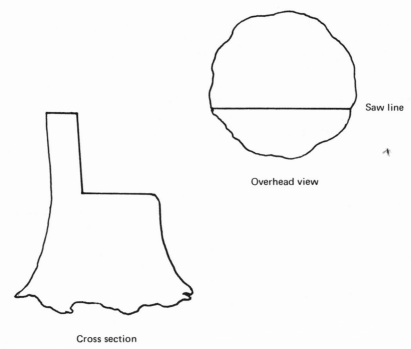

Saw line

Overhead view

Cross section

Fig. 3-3 *Bench created from tree stump*

done at ground or any other level that is convenient. Removing the inner bark prevents the tree from passing the food generated in the leaves down to the roots, which then starve, killing the tree.

Another method is to place an herbicide, such as ammate crystals, in notches made in the tree trunk with an ax. This method also kills the roots, as noted earlier.

TREE MAINTENANCE

Like all other well-selected vegetation in a natural landscape, trees should be the kind that do not require watering, fertilizing, or any other maintenance over an extended period. On occasion you may find, however, that you have to prune your trees to remove dead, dying, or unsightly limbs or branches. Sprouts growing at or near the base of the tree trunk and branches that cross or grow toward the center of the tree should be removed. A tree that forms a V-shaped

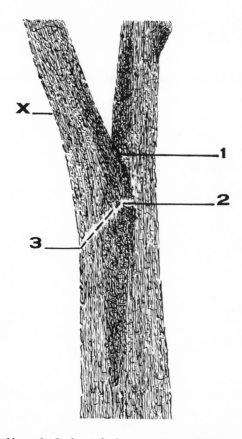

Fig. 3-4 *Cutting a V crotch. Stub cut the large member at X. The apparent juncture of the branches is at 1; the actual point of union is at 2. A cut from 3 to 2 gives the best surface for healing. U.S. Dept. of Agriculture, 1976.* Pruning Shade Trees and Repairing Their Injuries. *(Home & Garden Bulletin No. 83) Washington, D.C.*

crotch should have one of the sections forming the "v" removed because v-shaped crotches split easily, especially during storms.

Trees that normally develop one main stem will sometimes develop multiple ones. You may wish to prune these back to prod the tree into developing its normal shape. And of course you will want to remove branches that interfere with electrical or telephone wires, that shade street lights or interfere with traffic, that throw shade in the wrong place, or prevent cooling breezes in the summer.

An ordinary program of tree pruning may be undertaken by the average home owner, but a professional arborist should assist with the extraordinary jobs, especially felling large heavy limbs a significant distance above ground level. That kind of work is not for the amateur. The risks to life and limb are too great.

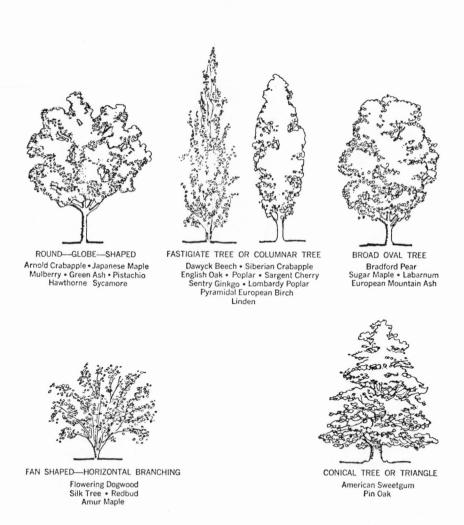

ROUND—GLOBE—SHAPED
Arnold Crabapple • Japanese Maple
Mulberry • Green Ash • Pistachio
Hawthorne Sycamore

FASTIGIATE TREE OR COLUMNAR TREE
Dawyck Beech • Siberian Crabapple
English Oak • Poplar • Sargent Cherry
Sentry Ginkgo • Lombardy Poplar
Pyramidal European Birch
Linden

BROAD OVAL TREE
Bradford Pear
Sugar Maple • Labarnum
European Mountain Ash

FAN SHAPED—HORIZONTAL BRANCHING
Flowering Dogwood
Silk Tree • Redbud
Amur Maple

CONICAL TREE OR TRIANGLE
American Sweetgum
Pin Oak

Figure 3-5

Fig. 3-6 *Plant growth regions of the United States*

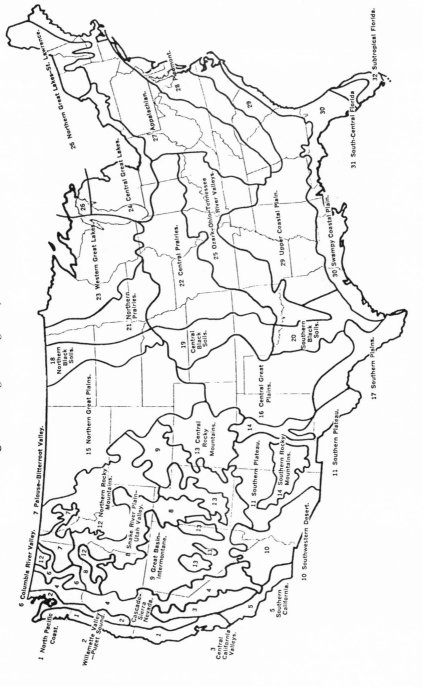

1 North Pacific Coast.
2 Willamette Valley—Puget Sound.
3 Central California Valleys.
4 Cascade-Sierra Nevada.
5 Southern California.
6 Columbia River Valley.
7 Palouse—Bitterroot Valley.
8 Snake River Plain—Utah Valley.
9 Great Basin-Intermontane.
10 Southwestern Desert.
11 Southern Plateau.
12 Northern Rocky Mountains.
13 Central Rocky Mountains.
14 Southern Rocky Mountains.
15 Northern Great Plains.
16 Central Great Plains.
17 Southern Plains.
18 Northern Black Soils.
19 Central Black Soils.
20 Southern Black Soils.
21 Northern Prairies.
22 Central Prairies.
23 Western Great Lakes.
24 Central Great Lakes.
25 Ozark-Ohio-Tennessee River Valleys.
26 Northern Great Lakes-St. Lawrence.
27 Appalachian.
28 Piedmont.
29 Upper Coastal Plain.
30 Swampy Coastal Plain.
31 South-Central Florida.
32 Subtropical Florida.

Fig. 3-7 *The flower of the flowering dogwood tree brings color to the spring landscape. (Photo by Dean M. Gottehrer)*

ADDING NEW TREES

Before selecting a new tree to place in your natural landscape, you should first attempt to see the living plant. You can visit an arboretum (which will also give you ideas about other trees you might wish to have), a nursery, a botanical garden, or a friend or neighbor who previously has planted such a tree. Be sure that the tree's characteristics match those you require, that its size at maturity will fill, but not crowd, the spot you have in mind, that its shape and branching habit is one you find pleasing, that it can tolerate the weather in your area, and that its flower, fruit, and fall colors fit in with other elements in your natural landscape.

The natural landscaper has a preference for native trees as well as other vegetation. The following list of noteworthy native trees was developed by the U.S. Department of Agriculture. The growth regions are keyed to the map on page 35.

Native Trees

Tree	Growth Region	Comment
Abies concolor (White fir)	4,5,9–14,27,28	Evergreen; shapely fine leaves
Acacia farnesiana (Huisache)	5,10,11,17,20,29,30	Grows larger with moisture
Acer rubrum (Red maple)	19–30	Rapid growing; red fall colors
Acer saccharum (Sugar maple)	2,15,18,21–29	Brilliant autumn colors
Aesculus glabra (Ohio buckeye)	22,24,25,27–29	—
Arbutus menziesi (Madroña)	1–3,5,10	Difficult to transplant
Carya species (Hickory)	20–30	Hard to transplant
Catalpa species (Catalpa)	21–23,25–30	Large leaves; showy flowers
Celtis occidentalis (Hackberry)	15–30	Drought resistant
Cercidium torreyanum (Palo-verde)	10–11	Excellent in desert
Chamaecyparis lawsoniana (Port Orford cedar)	1,2,28,29	70 varieties
Cornus florida (Flowering dogwood)	1,2,20,22–25,27–30	Pink, white, double flowers
Cornus nuttalli (Pacific dogwood)	1–5,12	Somewhat difficult to grow
Cupressus macrocarpa (Monterey cypress)	1,5	Highly picturesque
Fagus grandifolia (American beech)	20,22–30	Magnificent tree
Fraxinus americana (White ash)	20,22–25,27–30	—
Fraxinus pensylvanica (Red ash)	15,18,20	—
Gleditsia triacanthos (Honey locust)	16,20,22–30	Highly drought resistant
Ilex opaca (American holly)	20,25,27–30	Many varieties
Juglans species (Walnut)	18–30	—

Native Trees

Tree	Growth Region	Comment
Juniperus species (Red cedar)	4,12,22–24,26,27	Western mountains and East
Larix species (Larch)	1,4,5,29,30	—
Libocedrus decurrens (Incense cedar)	2,20,22,25,27–30	Elegant evergreen
Liquidambar styraciflua (Sweet gum)	2,21–29	Brilliant fall color
Liriodendron tulipifera (Tulip-tree)		Rapid growing
Lyonothamnus floribundus (Catalina ironwood)	5	—
Magnolia species (Magnolia)	1–3,5,25,27–30	Beautiful trees
Morus rubra (Red mulberry)	16–25,27–30	Attractive to birds
Nyssa sylvatica (Black gum)	20,22,24,25–30	Brilliant fall color
Oxydendrum arboreum (Sourwood)	25,27–30	Attractive in flower
Picea pungens (Blue spruce)	9,12–14,27–29	Exceptional form, color
Pinus species (Pine) About 40 species, use any native to your region.		
Platanus species (Sycamore)	3–5,10,11,16,20–22,24–30	Best in wet places with rich soil; majestic trees
Pseudotsuga menziesi (Douglas fir)	1–6,9,11,13,14,16,25,27–29	—
Quercus species (Oak)	At least one in every region	Slow-growing, superb, long-lived trees
Robinia pseudo-acacia (Black locust)	1–8,12,15,16,20–23,25–29	—
Sassafras albidum (Sassafras)	2,20,22–30	—
Sequoia sempervirens (Redwood)	1	Our tallest tree
Sequoiadendron giganteum (Sequoia)	4	Our most massive tree

Taxodium species (Cypress)	17,20,25,28–32	—
Thuja plicata (Western red cedar)	1,2,4,6,7,12	—
Tilia species (Basswood)	East, Southeast	Excellent shade trees
Tsuga canadensis (Canadian hemlock)	22,25,27–29	Excellent hedge
Tsuga heterophylla (Western hemlock)	1,2,4,6,12	—
Tsuga mertensiana (Mountain hemlock)	4,12	—
Ulmus americana (American elm)	1,2,15,16,18–23,25–30	—
Washingtonia species (Palm)	Southwest generally	—
Yucca species (Yucca)	Southwest	Desert gardens

One of the most important functions trees serve in the natural landscape is providing shade. The U.S. Department of Agriculture has developed the following lists of shade trees noted for their specific characteristics. The zones noted refer to the map on page 22 and are the coldest ones where the trees are hardy.

Recommended Small Shade Trees

Tree	Zone	Tree	Zone
Acer buergerianum (Trident maple)	6	*Cornus florida* (Flowering dogwood)	4
Acer carpinifolium (Hornbeam maple)	5	*Elaeagnus angustifolia* (Russian olive)	2
Acer japonicum (Fullmoon maple)	5	*Fraxinus holotricha* (Balkan ash)	5
Acer mandshuricum (Manchurian maple)	4	*Fraxinus ornus* (Flowering ash)	5
Acer nikoense (Nikko maple)	5	*Koelreuteria paniculata* (Golden-rain tree)	5
Carpinus Betulus 'Globosa' (European hornbeam)	5	*Magnolia soulangeana* (Saucer magnolia)	2
Carpinus caroliniana (American hornbeam)	2	*Oxydendrum arboreum* (Sourwood)	5
Cercis canadensis (Eastern redbud)	4	*Ulmus parvifolia* (Chinese elm)	5

Recommended Large Shade Trees

Tree	Zone	Tree	Zone
Acer rubrum (Red maple)	3	*Quercus alba* (White oak)	4
Acer saccharum (Sugar maple)	3	*Quercus borealis* (Northern red oak)	3
Fagus sylvatica (European beech)	4	*Quercus palustris* (Pin oak)	4
Liriodendron tulipifera (Tulip-tree)	4	*Tilia cordata* (Little-leaf linden)	3
Magnolia acuminata (Cucumber tree)	4		

Recommended Shade Trees for Wet Soils

Tree	Zone	Tree	Zone
Acer rubrum (Red maple)	3	*Nyssa sylvatica* (Black tupelo)	4
Liquidambar styraciflua (Sweet gum)	5	*Quercus bicolor* (Swamp white oak)	3
Magnolia virginiana (Sweet bay)	5		

Recommended Shade Trees for Dry Soils and Urban Areas

Tree	Zone	Tree	Zone
Betula davurica (Dahlurian birch)	4	*Quercus acutissima* (Sawtooth oak)	6
Fraxinus pensylvanica (Seedless green ash)	2	*Quercus kelloggi* (California black oak)	7
Fraxinus velutina (Velvet ash)	5	*Sassafras albidum* (Sassafras)	4
Koelreuteria paniculata (Golden-rain tree)	5	*Sophora japonica* (Japanese pagoda tree)	4

Shade Trees Not Recommended

Tree	Zone	Tree	Zone
Acer saccharinum (Silver maple)	3	*Ginkgo biloba* (Ginkgo [female])	4
Aesculus Hippocastanum (Horse-chestnut)	3	*Morus alba* (White mulberry)	4
		Populus species(Poplar)	1–8
Ailanthus altissima (Tree-of-Heaven)	4	*Salix babylonica* (Weeping willow)	6
		Ulmus americana (American elm)	2

Shade Trees Relatively Free of Insect or Disease Pests

Tree	Zone	Tree	Zone
Carpinus caroliniana (American hornbeam)	2	*Laburnum alpinum* (Scotch laburnum)	4
Cercidiphyllum japonicum (Katsura tree)	4	*Liquidambar styraciflua* (Sweet gum)	5
		Ostrya virginiana (Hop-hornbeam)	4
Cladrastis lutea (American yellow-wood)	3	*Phellodendron amurense* (Amur cork-tree)	3
Cornus mas (Cornelian cherry)	3	*Sophora japonica* (Japanese pagoda tree)	4
Ginkgo biloba (Maidenhair tree [male])	4		
Koelreuteria paniculata (Golden-rain tree)	5		

Recommended Shade Trees with Colored Leaves Two or More Seasons

Tree	Zone	Leaf color
Acer japonicum "Aureum" (Fullmoon maple)	5	Yellow

Recommended Shade Trees with Colored Leaves Two or More Seasons

Tree	Zone	Leaf color
Acer palmatum "Atropurpureum" (Japanese maple)	5	Red
Acer platanoides "Crimson King" (Norway maple)	3	Red
Acer pseudo-platanus "Purpureum" (Purple-leaf sycamore maple)	5	Purple
Elaeagnus angustifolia (Russian olive)	2	Gray
Fagus sylvatica "Purpureo-pendula" (Weeping purple beech)	4	Purple
Quercus Robur "Concordia" (Golden Oak)	5	Yellow
Tilia tomentosa (Silver linden)	4	Gray

Shade Trees with Unusual Bark

Tree	Zone	Bark
Acer griseum (Paperbark maple)	5	Cinnamon-brown; peels off
Acer pensylvanicum (Striped maple)	3	Green and white striped
Betula alba-sinensis (Chinese paper birch)	5	Bright orange; peels off longitudinally
Carpinus caroliniana (American hornbeam)	2	Gray; "muscled" trunk
Elaeagnus angustifolia (Russian olive)	2	Brown; shreds longitudinally
Phellodendron amurense (Amur cork-tree)	3	Mature; corky
Prunus serrulata (Red bark cherry)	5	Brilliant glossy red

BUSHES AND SHRUBS 4

The clipping of plants into hedges and grotesque forms is mechanical, and the plant has been deprived of its freedom to grow into its full beauty. The skill of the landscaper lies in his ability to find the plant which need not be maimed and distorted to fit the situation.

Jens Jensen, *Siftings*, 1939

The beauty of the desert-blooming ocotillo, the pinkish-purple rhododendrons that blanket the Smoky Mountains, the blue banks of ceanothus that paint California hillsides, the flame-colored azaleas that invigorate the Deep South and add life to New England's spring, the intriguing flowers of the mountain laurel, even the heather-covered moors of England—all remind us of the beauty a flowering bush brings into our lives.

Food and shelter.   Shrubs and bushes protect the soil from the eroding effects of rain, wind, and snow. They also shelter areas from the sun and provide barriers to noise and, if tall enough, to wind. Shrubs can change the climate conditions in their immediate vicinity by increasing the humidity and reducing the extremes of temperature, making the area warmer in winter and cooler in summer.

Shrubs and bushes are important in the management of wildlife in the natural landscape. The fruit adds to the diet of local wildlife and their leaves and twigs are food for mammals such as deer and rabbits. They also provide a quick escape for wild animals such as the grey squirrel, or the jackrabbit who must make a hasty departure into the nearest sagebrush away from the clutches of an aggressive coyote.

The berries, aside from feeding the birds and other animals, are also sought after by humans—blueberries, raspberries, and others for eating, bay berries for making bayberry candles, the fruit of cactus for making cactus candy and of beach plums for beach plum jelly. Bushes and shrubs can also be an important source of honey.

Fig. 4-1 *A desert cactus in bloom (Photo by Dean M. Gottehrer)*

Structure and design.   In the natural landscape shrubs and bushes can be used to structure the grounds, provide a background for other plants, or decorate the landscape. They can structure the grounds by dividing the land into different areas—for play, for service and composting, or for separating one kind of plant from another. The highly pruned and sculptured hedges of formal landscape design divided land for different uses in the past. These hedges are to be avoided in the natural landscape because they simply aren't natural. But many of the same plants can still be used if they are allowed to grow naturally, without formal pruning. Be sure to place them so their mature size fills the given space without crowding other plants or dominating and overwhelming the design.

Shrubs provide a background for flower beds. They soften the contrast between tall trees and low-growing plants. They can also be used to soften the outlines of your house, accent a window or door, create a boundary along the driveway, provide a focus of interest along an otherwise empty wall, and add color and fragrance to the natural landscape in spring and summer. Shrubs can be placed to provide privacy or to block ugly or displeasing views.

Fig. 4-2 *The art of topiary hedge sculpting has been highly refined at Disneyland, but these artificially created designs have no place in the natural landscape. (Photo by Dean M. Gottehrer)*

SHRUB INVENTORY

Inventory your shrubs before you make any changes. Live with them for at least a year before you decide you don't like any particular one. In the course of the seasons they may reveal something beautiful and charming, something worth preserving.

After you have inventoried your shrubs and bushes, determine what functions they now perform in your landscape. Do they add privacy, shade the house or some part of the garden, delineate boundaries between your property and your neighbor's or mark off different areas of your grounds for different uses? Do they provide a beautiful sight in spring or summer when they bloom? Do animals use them for shelter, food, or protection?

SHRUB REMOVAL

Once you have answered these questions you can examine which shrubs or bushes you want to eliminate and which you will keep. Never eliminate the last plant of any kind until you have determined beyond a shadow of a doubt that you do not want it.

Bushes and shrubs can be cut down, afterwards the roots should be pulled out. Or you can kill both shrub and roots with an herbicide such as ammate. It is as important to kill all the roots of an established and hardy shrub as it is to kill the roots of a tree. Otherwise the plant will begin to grow again. Sometimes it is difficult to kill all the shrub roots because it is easy to overlook some of them, especially if you have cut the bush down first.

If you have natural shrublands on your property don't touch them—don't remove any plants, don't add any plants. Too much of this precious natural resource is being destroyed to clear land for housing developments, suburban shopping malls, and office buildings. Help preserve this type of natural vegetation by doing nothing that would alter its presence or beauty.

SHRUB MAINTENANCE

Select bushes and shrubs that are hardy, tough, and pest-free and your maintenance chores will be limited to pruning. Some pruning is always inevitable, but it can be kept to a minimum if you choose bushes and shrubs with a growth pattern that fits the allotted space. It is extremely difficult to hold back a naturally large shrub or bush and it is nearly impossible to stimulate a small bush or shrub to grow larger than its usual size. Although, within certain limits of the plant's potential, it can be done, it is far less work to choose the proper size and shape beforehand.

To produce flowers, pruning is necessary with almost all shrubs since most shrubs flower on new growth. Shrubs that flower in the spring do so on new growth from the previous summer. These plants should be pruned immediately after they flower so that the new growth has time to mature and harden before winter. Shrubs that flower in the summer and fall do so on new growth from that spring. These shrubs should not be pruned immediately after they flower because that would encourage new growth that would not be hardy enough to make it through the winter. Late-blooming plants should be pruned in early spring after any frost danger has passed. In warmer sections of the country, it is possible to prune in the fall or winter, but it is best to wait until the bush is dormant.

Newly planted shrubs can be cut back nearly to the ground to improve their growth. If they are purchased with their roots canned or with the rootball placed in burlap, only a little pruning is necessary.

Fig. 4-3 *Bushes and shrubs in a natural landscape design by Jens Jensen (Courtesy of Leonard K. Eaton and University of Michigan, College of Agriculture Library)*

Shrubs that produce new growth from near the ground each year before they flower generally will improve if some of their canes are cut back to the ground each year. It is also wise to prune drastically an old shrub that hasn't been pruned for years. If the shrub is one that flowers from growth that is several years old, then the cutting-back process should take two or three years to complete, cutting back a fraction of the old growth each year. If the bush blooms on growth that comes up each succeeding year, the drastic pruning can be done all at once.

Some bushes and shrubs are special pruning cases. You should consult experts before taking action if you have any doubts about what you are planning to cut back. Additional advice may be found in books listed in the bibliography.

ADDING NEW SHRUBS

After removing unwanted bushes and shrubs, you may want to add some new ones. Additional shrubs should be chosen for the part they will play in your landscape. An evergreen, such as mountain laurel, can be planted near any tree windbreaks you have established. The bush will provide a windbreak closer to the ground and add to the savings and advantages of the windbreak. In the case of the mountain laurel you will also have beautiful flowers in the early summer.

An informal hedge may fit your landscape design and perform a valuable function in your natural landscape. Forsythia, azaleas, and rhododendrons are just a few of the plants you can use in an informal hedge. Since the plants will not be pruned to a sculptured shape, it is important to place them so they will have enough space and will not be crowded. Avoid straight lines in your informal hedge. Plant shrubs in sweeping curves of irregularly shaped masses for a more natural effect. Informal hedges need less pruning and trimming and can include a greater variety of bushes and shrubs than a formal hedge. Plant shrubs and bushes that will attain the form you want your hedge to take when it is fully grown. Take your time to find the bushes and shrubs that are the size, shape, and appearance that you want in your informal hedge. For the minimum-maintenance landscape, choose your shrubs and bushes with care because otherwise they will be second only to a lawn in the attention they require. Obtain young plants, since they adapt more readily, and shear them in the early years to stimulate a denser growth at the base. This will save time in the long run since the denser growth will discourage weeds.

Consider visibility when placing a new shrub or bush. If privacy is your goal, you will want to obscure visibility—of your house from the neighbors or the road, of the service area from yourself or your guests, or of a view you don't find pleasing. However, you want to encourage visibility for cars driving on the road and from your own car as you enter or leave the driveway. Don't plant bushes and shrubs near a drive or roadway where they will obscure visibility.

Don't place bushes and shrubs too close to the house. A bush that is in contact with the side of the house can rot the boards of a wooden house. Leave enough room for air to circulate between the plant when it is full grown and the house and also enough room for maintenance of the plant or the house. The tendency is to leave too little room between plants in the attempt to create the appearance of fully grown plants. Leave adequate space between shrubs and bushes for later growth and in the early years fill the spaces with flowers or other small plants.

When choosing new bushes and shrubs to add to your natural landscape, first look at those known to be local favorites. They are the ones that usually have proven themselves to be good healthy plants—the types that appeal to the natural landscaper. Then consider size, shape, foliage texture, limb and twig patterns of growth when the plant is leafless, how the bush or shrub will fit into the pattern of flowering and fruiting succession, the color, fragrance, and fruit the shrub produces, and the general suitability to the conditions available—soil, moisture, sun, shade, and wind.

Bushes come in a variety of shapes—round, oval, ovate (a bush that is broadest below the middle), obovate (a bush that is broadest above the middle), broader than high, conical, columnar, and irregular. Shrubs and bushes also have a variety of branching patterns including upright-narrow to spreading, upright-arching, horizontal, pendulous, and irregular. Shapes and branching patterns are especially important if you have a space of a certain shape that you wish to fill.

Some shrubs grow well only in acid soil. These include all the azaleas, both evergreen and deciduous, rhododendrons, mountain laurel, camellias, blueberries, heathers, and Scotch brooms.

Evergreen shrubs, such as juniper and Japanese yew, often form foundation plantings around many homes. The reason is simple. They grow very slowly, need almost no maintenance once they are established, and provide a splash of green during the winter months when trees and bushes have shed their foliage. Some of these plants have become landscaping clichés—seen everywhere without thought to their specific virtues. Like all clichés they originally served a valuable function. Since they are low-maintenance plants, they are to be valued in the natural landscape. However, they should be used sparingly and with forethought. If another plant will serve the same function, use it. Include evergreen shrubs in your natural landscape only when no other plants will accomplish the same goal.

Be certain that the prospective bush or shrub has become adapted to the environment if it is not locally native. Pay close attention to whether it will make it through the winter without damage from early or late freezing.

The U.S. Department of Agriculture has prepared a list of 40 shrubs that will flourish in the natural landscape since they are tough, require little maintenance, and have few or no pest problems. The zones are keyed to the map on page 22.

Selected Shrubs

Shrub	Zone	Flower Colors	Flower Season
Abelia grandiflora (Glossy abelia)	5	Pink	August
Acanthopanax sieboldianus (Aralia)	4	—	—
Arbutus Unedo (Strawberry tree)	8	White	Winter
Aronia arbutifolia (Red chokeberry)	4	White-to-red	Late May
Berberis thunbergi (Japanese barberry)	4	Yellow; reddish	Mid-May
Buxus microphylla japonica (Japanese boxwood)	5	—	—
Camellia japonica (in variety) (Camellia)	7	White-to-red	Oct.–April
Chionanthus virginicus (Fringe-tree)	4	White	Early June
Clethra alnifolia (Summer-sweet)	3	White	Late July
Deutzia gracilis (Slender deutzia)	4	White	Late May
Elaeagnus angustifolia (Russian olive)	2	Silver and yellow	Early June
Euonymus alatus (Burning-bush)	3	—	—
Forsythia intermedia (Forsythia)	5	Yellow	Mid-April
Fothergilla monticola (Alabama fothergilla)	5	White	Mid-May
Hamamelis mollis (Chinese witch-hazel)	5	Yellow	March
Hibiscus Rosa-sinensis (Chinese hibiscus)	9	White, pink, red	Summer
Hibiscus syriacus (Shrubby althaea)	5	White-to-blue	August
Hypericum patulum henryi (Henry St. John's-wort)	6	Yellow	July
Ilex crenata (Japanese holly)	6	Inconspicuous	Late June
Juniperus chinensis pfitzeriana (Pfitzer juniper)	4	—	—

Kalmia latifolia (Mountain laurel)	4	Pink and white	Mid-June
Kolkwitzia amabilis (Beauty-bush)	4	Pink	Early June
Lagerstroemia indica (Crape-myrtle)	7	Pink-to-red	August
Lonicera tatarica (Tatarian honeysuckle)	3	Pink-to-white	Late May
Nerium oleander (Oleander)	7–8	White, yellow-to-red and purple	Apr. through summer
Philadelphus coronarius (Mock-orange)	4	White	Early June
Pieris japonica (Japanese andromeda)	5	Creamy white	Mid-April
Pittosporum Tobira (Japanese pittosporum)	8	Creamy white	May
Potentilla fruticosa (Bush cinquefoil)	2	Yellow-to-white	Mid-May to Sept.
Raphiolepis indica (Indian hawthorn)	8	Pinkish	May
Rhododendron (in variety) (Rhododendron and azalea)	2	Various	April–July
Rhodotypos scandens (Jetbead)	5	White	Mid-May
Rhus copallina (Shining sumac)	4	Greenish	Early August
Rosa rugosa (Rugosa rose)	2	Pink-to-white	Early June
Spirea Bumalda (Bumalda spirea)	5	Crimson	Late June–July
Spirea vanhouttei (Vanhoutte spirea)	4	White	Late May
Taxus cuspidata (Japanese yew)	4	—	—
Viburnum carlcephalum (Fragrant snowball)	5	White	Late May
Viburnum plicatum Mariesi (Maries doublefile viburnum)	4	White	Late May
Xanthorhiza simplicissima (Yellowroot)	4	Brownish-purple	Early May

Fig. 4-4 *Azaleas bring a burst of color to spring landscapes. (Photo by Dean M. Gottehrer)*

Fig. 4-5 *Leaves of a holly (Photo by Dean M. Gottehrer)*

Fig. 4-6 *The flowers of the mountain laurel come into bloom after rhododendrons and azaleas (Photo by Dean M. Gottehrer)*

Fig. 4-7 *The hydrangea bush produces prolific blooms. (Photo by Dean M. Gottehrer)*

Native Shrubs

Shrub	*Growth Region*	*Comment*
Artemisia tridentata (Sagebrush)	2,4–13,15,27,28	Fine, silver-white bush; requires alkaline soil
Ceanothus impressus (Santa Barbara ceanothus)	5, possibly 29,30	Dark blue flowers
Chionanthus virginicus (Fringe-tree)	1–3,20,22,24,25,27–30	Lacy, white, fragrant flowers
Cordia boissieri (Anacahuita)	11,17,30, possibly 29–32	Very rare evergreen
Fremontia mexicana (Flannel-bush)	5	Waxy yellow flowers
Hydrangea quercifolia (Oakleaf hydrangea)	1,2,24,25,28–30	Large panicles of white flowers
Ilex vomitoria (Yaupon)	20,28–30 (probably 1–3, 5)	Evergreen; profuse red berries
Kalmia latifolia (Mountain laurel)	1,2,24–30	Pink-white flowers; evergreen
Larrea tridentata (Creosote bush)	9–11,16,17	Yellow-flowered; desert shrub
Mahonia Aquifolium (Oregon grape)	1,2,4,6,7,11–16,22,24,25,27–29	Bright yellow flowers; blue grapelike fruits
Rhododendron calendulaceum (Flame azalea)	1,2,3,20,22,24,25,27–29	Brilliant flowers; finest native ornamental
Sophora secundiflora (Mescal bean)	11,16,17,20,29,30	Violet-blue; fragrant flowers
Stewartia ovata grandiflora (Mountain stewartia)	1,2,20,22,24,25,27–30	Waxy white flowers up to 4" across
Viburnum trilobum (Cranberry bush)	1,2,4,12,13,15,18,21,27	White flat-topped flowers; bright red fruits

Fig. 4-8 *A rhododendron in blossom (Photo by Dean M. Gottehrer)*

Native shrubs also have their place in the natural landscape. The U.S. Department of Agriculture has a list of noteworthy native shrubs. The growth region is keyed to the map on page 35.

Other lists of shrubs and bushes as well as instructions for planting can be found in some of the books in the bibliography.

LAWNS AND 5
OTHER
GROUND COVERS

A little meadow covered with flowers, over which butterflies play and bees hum, is in itself a scene that becomes dearer and dearer as a man grows older; and its power often becomes so great that it draws him back to his home of boyhood days once again to drink of the beauty of this meadow and to seek the little brook which carries his thoughts with its current toward the river, and from the river toward the sea, and across the sea to other continents.

Jens Jensen, *Siftings*, 1939

A green velvet carpet to welcome the weary and comfort the family, a piece of soft green flannel cut to the contours of the landscape and glued to the earth—these are images of the American dream of the perfect lawn. One critic has called it "a living fossil in a modern human zoo."

Lawns. The first lawn probably evolved from the grazing, trampling, and excremental habits of animals kept outside the front door. The animals—cattle, sheep, and goats—ate enough of the wild grasses to keep them closely cropped. As they grazed they trampled the grass underfoot, reduced the woody growth to a minimum, and compacted the soil. Their excrement fertilized the lawn, which grew lush and beautiful. The result was cheap and easy to maintain.

Remove the animals, however, and the costs skyrocket. Instead of wild grasses growing, new grass must be planted. Instead of animals compacting the soil, the earth must now be rolled. Instead of manure returning the nutrients from the grass back to the soil, chemical fertilizers must maintain the lush growth. In place of grazing animals cropping the grass, the lawn must be cut by a power mower. What was once virtually free and required little effort has now become a costly, time-consuming chore. In a sense, there is no more expensive crop grown in the world than a lawn, which must be mowed, watered, trimmed, fertilized, sprayed with herbicides and pesticides to remove weeds and animal pests, and yet yields neither food nor flowers.

There are functions that grass does perform. A lawn turf is created by tiller grasses—those which grow to the side by sending out stems along the ground. Grass has fine fibrous roots. Together with the stems and leaves, the roots do an excellent job of protecting the soil. Grass prevents the soil from blowing away when it is dry and from washing away in a summer squall. The roots keep the soil porous, soaking up water and reducing runoff. This stabilizes the water table and cleans and filters surface waters. Unfortunately the cost of maintaining the grassy lawn is out of proportion to the benefits derived. The same functions can be performed by other plants that don't require nearly as much attention and care. There are, however, a number of places where grass is the best ground cover for practical or aesthetic reasons.

As an edge along roadways, sidewalks, and other pathways, grass is likely to be preferred. Green grass provides a color contrast with the edge of the road to guide drivers. It lessens the chances of ragged road edges while it stabilizes the roadside soil. Grass is a safe surface upon which to leave the road in an emergency and also can serve as an extra parking area when you have a large number of visitors. Grass will not be damaged if snow is piled on it during street cleaning in the winter. Along sidewalks and pathways, including bikeways, grass provides a low-level ground cover that will not suffer from occasional traffic. In all of these border uses, properly trimmed grass provides good visibility.

The front lawn is the approach to the house. It allows residents and guests to see the house and appreciate it in its formal perspective. The side and back lawns often are used as recreational areas by the family. One writer has stated that a lawn between one-quarter and one-half an acre requires a riding mower, over one-half an acre requires a tractor with a mowing attachment, and only a lawn that is less than 750 square feet (the equivalent of a plot 25 by 30 feet) can be maintained by a hand-operated reel mower. A walk through suburbia will bear witness that reel mowers have gone the way of manual can openers—still around, but hardly used anymore.

In the natural landscape, areas devoted to lawns should be small enough to mow with a hand mower. Let use dictate the size of the

Fig. 5-1 *Winter aspect with naturalistic little bluestem grassland (foreground) surrounding the narrow strip of lawn next to the house. (Courtesy Connecticut Arboretum)*

lawn you plant. A few feet of lawn around the house will set the house off from its surroundings and also prevent the spread of brush fires. A small lawn, well-designed, will provide adequate space for picnics and lawn games.

The meadow.   What should be done with the space formerly occupied by the lawn? As suggested in Chapter Two, let the grass grow. Create a meadow in your backyard. Let the lawn become a grassland. You can't create a natural grassland, of course, because that would require herds of buffalo and other trampling grazing animals as well as fires to keep the growth down. Warren G. Kenfield tells us:

> *The Grassland is a thing of beauty. As the season advances from early spring to late fall, one grass after another becomes prominent, in green, yellow, pink, and bronze. Each in time waves in the breezes like the proverbial field of wheat—except that a field of wheat is a mighty poor substitute for the real thing.*
>
> *Furthermore, the Grassland is not just a blanket of green, as monotonous as your lawn. It is a tapestry studded with flowers. From*

Fig. 5-2 *The back "lawn" mostly converted to a wild grassland. Orchard grass is in foreground with several clumps of hardy iris (one clump center foreground, others beyond). Near the house pitch pine (left), gray birch, mountain laurel (flowering), red cedars, blue spruce, and weeping cherry have been set within or around a narrow strip of lawn. (Courtesy Connecticut Arboretum)*

the earliest spring bulbs to the last chrysanthemums they come and go in endless profusion. Sometimes there will be a lowlying carpet of yellow, extending continuously. Then there will be the isolated orange of lilies and the purple spikes of blazing star, or patches of asters and goldenrods. As one vanishes (literally vanishes, without benefit of gardening) another bursts into view. Finally, all turns to magnificent hues of brown in the autumn frosts. It is submerged beneath a sea of snow. It emerges with spring thaws as smooth as if flattened by some conscientious roller.

Warren G. Kenfield, *The Wild Gardener in the Wild Landscape*, 1966

Creating your own meadow does not mean that you have finished forever taking care of that space. It only means that you have given up regular mowing, fertilizing, watering, rolling, and spraying to get rid of weeds. You may want to mow a pathway through it every so often. You will still have to be careful to prevent any unwanted vegetation from getting a foothold—depending on where you live,

Fig. 5-3 *Viewed from close up, the dandelion radiates a beauty all its own. (Photo by Dean M. Gottehrer)*

you may find that woody plants will attempt to invade. The solution is simple. On your walks through your meadow, as you are communing with nature, pull out any woody growth or tree seedlings that you don't want taking over. You might also want to hurry nature along a bit by planting some wildflowers in the meadow. See Chapter Eight for details on wildflowers and how to obtain them.

In the beginning, as you are letting your meadow grow, you should tolerate what you previously perceived as weeds. You won't get rid of everything you thought of as weeds right away and may never eliminate some plants you don't want. The thing to do is to see them differently. Dandelion flowers are not as despicable as you might think—and they will probably cease to be a problem. Have you ever seen a meadow full of dandelions? Probably not. As wild plants grow, they tend to crowd out such plants as dandelions, sending them into nearby lawns.

Other ground covers.   Another way to eliminate or reduce the size of your lawn is to replace the grass with other types of ground covers. In traditional home landscaping, ground covers have always been problem solvers. In the shade, on steep banks, in soil extremely wet or extremely dry, properly selected ground covers will always flourish.

Fig. 5-4 *The dandelion seed head carries this plant to all corners of your lawn. (Photo by Dean M. Gottehrer)*

They can also be used to replace the lawn entirely, but only when the following advantages of grass are not important to the natural landscape. First, grass can be cut to a uniform height, usually between one and two inches depending on the type of grass. Most ground covers are not so domesticated and will seek their own height, although some will benefit from an occasional pruning or even cutting back almost to ground level. Secondly, no ground cover will take the abuse of people walking on it continuously. Only grass can take such constant abuse and not show irreparable damage. So, if the areas where you contemplate replacing lawn with ground cover need uniform height or toughness to withstand traffic abuse, don't make the change. But if you have places where the lawn is only decorative or serves just as a background that is rarely walked on, then you can exchange the grass for another type of ground cover.

Some ground covers have advantages over grass. Ground covers such as the myrtles, sedums, phloxes, and St. John's-wort have bright flowers. Others, including the cotoneasters, coralberry, and bearberry, have brightly colored fruits. And still others are evergreens that provide a year-round accent to the natural landscape.

Some ground covers, such as pachysandra, offer several advantages. Pachysandra grows well under most trees. It thrives in the

Fig. 5-5 *Bearberry*

shade and enjoys the dropping leaves in fall. Dr. Richard Goodwin tells of an area around his mother's home that was planted in pachysandra underneath the shade of a few oak trees nearly fifty years ago. In all that time, nothing was done to maintain the pachysandra. Today it still covers nearly 2,000 square feet around the house, absorbs the annual leaf fall from the oak trees, and transforms the leaves into black mulch on which the plants thrive.

ADDING NEW GROUND COVERS

When you decide to plant new ground covers, look at some examples of what you are considering before you actually plant them. Ground covers have different growing characteristics. Some are fast growers.

Fig. 5-6 *Bergenia*

The wintercreepers can begin with one plant and will cover several square feet in a few years. Others grow much more slowly and take their time to fill in. Some ground covers require more maintenance than others, although none of them demands as much attention as a lawn. Determine the full-grown size of any ground cover you choose before adding it to your natural landscape. Make sure it will fill the space you wish it to occupy. Talk with someone in your area who has used it and find out firsthand what the local experience with it has been.

Include areas of bulb plants along with new ground covers. Lilies, narcissus, and other bulbs do very well planted in with the ground cover. Take care to match the heights of the bulb plants and the ground cover so that the ground cover does not overshadow the bulb plants.

Fig. 5-7 *Galax*

Fig. 5-8 *Heather*

The guide to ground cover selection below, prepared by the U.S. Department of Agriculture, will give you ideas about ground covers you might consider. The hardiness zones are keyed to the map on page 22. Books listed in the bibliography provide additonal lists and information about planting and propagation.

Selected Ground Covers

Ground Cover	Height (Inches)	Hardiness Zone	Type	Soil and Light	Comments
Epimedium Species (Barrenwort)	12	4–8	Woody herb	Almost any soil	Dense foliage into winter; white, yellow, lavender flowers
Arctostaphylos Uva-ursi (Bearberry)	6–10	2–9	Evergreen shrub	Excellent in stony, sandy, acid soils	Low, hard to transplant; bright red fruit
Bergenia cordifolia (Bergenia, heartleaf)	12	5–10	Creeping perennial	Sun or partial shade	Pink flowers; thick heavy foliage
Genista pilosa; G. sagittalis (Broom)	6–12	5–9	Deciduous shrub	Well-drained soil; sun	Pea-shaped flowers
Ajuga reptans (Bugleweed)	4–8	5–9	Perennial herb	Tolerates most soils	Densely packed plants; rapid grower; blue-purple flowers
Phyla nodiflora (Capeweed)	2–4	9–10	Creeping perennial herb	Sand and waste areas	Low growing; spreads rapidly; light pink flowers
Symphoricarpos orbiculatus (Coralberry)	to 36	3–9	Deciduous shrub	Thrives in poor soils	Rapid growth underground stems; needs yearly pruning
Cotoneaster adpressa (Cotoneaster)	6–30	5–10	Semi-evergreen shrub	Full sun	Stems will layer; subject to fire blight
Vaccinium Vitis-Idaea (Cowberry)	to 12	5–9	Small evergreen shrub	Acid soil	Small pink flowers; dark-red berries
Liriope spicata (Creeping lily-turf)	to 12	5–10	Matted herb	Extreme heat; dry soil; stands salt spray	Dense mat; dark green leaves; purple flowers

Ground Cover	Height (Inches)	Hardiness Zone	Type	Soil and Light	Comments
Phyla nodiflora var. canescens (Creeping lippia)	2–4	5–10	Creeping perennial	Any soil; sun	White lilac flowers
Thymus Serpyllum (Creeping thyme)	to 3	5–10	Subshrub, creeping stems	Tolerates dry soils; sun	Substitute for grass
Coronilla varia (Crown vetch)	12–24	3–7	Herb	Dry; steep banks; sun	Rapid growing; small pink flowers
Hemerocallis species (Daylily)	18–60	3–10	Root; fleshy; tuber	Sun; dry to boggy soils	Summer flowers
Dichondra repens (Dichondra)	1–2	9, 10	Evergreen perennial	Sunny or shady locations	Rapid spreader
Sasa pumila (Dwarf bamboo)		6–10	Low shrub	Sun; sandy soil	Grass substitute; foliage brown in winter
Hedera Helix (English ivy)	6–8	5–9	Evergreen vine	Sun or shade	Clip leaves to control leaf spots
Forsythia species (Forsythia)	Trim to 18	5–9	Deciduous shrub	Sun; well-drained soil	Yellow spring flowers
Galax aphylla (Galax)	6	5–7	Evergreen; stemless perennial herb	Moist, rich, acid soil; shade	White spring flowers; bronze leaves in fall
Teucrium Chamaedrys (Germander)	to 10	6–10	Woody perennial	Sun or partial shade	Protect in winter
Glecoma hederacea (Ground-ivy)	3	3–9	Trailing perennial	Sun or shade; any soil	Forms low mat
Erica carnea (Heath)	6–12	5–8	Evergreen shrub	Poor acid soils; sun	Pink, purple, red types
Calluna vulgaris (Heather)	6–24	4–7	Evergreen shrub	Acid well-drained soil	Shear plants each spring

Name	Height	Zones	Type	Conditions	Notes
Ilex crenata (Japanese Holly)	to 24	6–10	Evergreen shrub	Sun or semi-shade	Slow growing; small bank
Mahonia repens (Hollygrape, dwarf)	to 10	6–9	Evergreen shrub	Sun or shade; any soil	Yellow flowers
Lonicera japonica (Honeysuckle, Japanese)	to 10	5–9	Twisting trailing vine	Sun or partial shade	Prune yearly to keep in bounds; semi-evergreen
Cephalophyllum; Carpobrotus; Delosperma; Drosanthemum; Malephora; Lampranthus (Ice-plant)	4–6	10	Low succulent	Sun; well-drained soil	Temporary ground cover in cold climates; brilliant colored flowers
Pachysandra terminalis (Japanese spurge)	to 6	5–8	Evergreen herb	Semi-shade under tree	Spreads underground stems
Juniperus horizontalis (Juniper)	12–18	3–10	Evergreen conifer	Sun; dry areas	Yearly pruning; wide range of colors
Lantana selloviana; L. montevidensis (Lantana)	6–10	8–10	Trailing shrub	Sun; high salt tolerance	Wide range of flower colors
Convallaria majalis (Lily-of-the-valley)	6–10	4–9	Rootstock	Rich, moist, high organic soil; partial shade	Fragrant white bell-shaped flowers
Ophiopogon japonicus (Lily-turf, dwarf; mondograss)	to 10	7–10	Matted herb	Any soil; sun or shade	Spikes of pale lilac flowers
Arenaria verna (Moss sandwort)	3	2–9	Perennial herb	Fertile, moist soil; shade	Protect in winter
Phlox subulata (Moss pink)	6	4–10	Evergreen perennial	Porous soil; sun	Pink and white flowers
Vinca minor, small leaves; *V. major*, large leaves (Periwinkle)	6–8	5–10	Trailing herb	Avoid high nitrogen fertilizer; poorly drained soils	Purple, blue, and white flowers

Ground Cover	Height (Inches)	Hardiness Zone	Type	Soil and Light	Comments
Hosta species (Plantain-lily)	12–16	4–10	Broad-leafed tufted plant	Moist well-drained soils; shade	Needs frequent division
Polygonum cuspidatum var. *compactum* (Polygonum, dwarf)	12–24	4–10	Stout perennial	Rocky or gravelly soil; sun	Foliage turns red in fall
Rosa wichuraiana (Rose, memorial)	6–12	5–9	Semi-evergreen low growing shrub	Banks and sand dunes	2-inch white flowers
Hypericum calycinum (St. John's-wort)	9–12	6–10	Semi-evergreen shrub	Semi-shade; sandy soil	Yellow flowers in summer; red fall foliage
Fragaria chiloensis (Sand strawberry)	10–12	6–10	Perennial herb	Suitable most soils	Spreads rapidly
Sarcococca hookeriana (Sarococca)	to 72	6–10	Evergreen shrub	Shade	Control height; large leaves; white flowers
Gazania rigens (South African daisy)	6–9	9–10	Evergreen perennial	Avoid high nitrogen fertilizers; poorly drained soils	Light green foliage; orange flowers
Sedum acre (Stonecrop, goldmoss)	4	4–10	Evergreen perennial	Dry areas	Forms mats of tiny foliage
Saxifraga sarmentosa (Strawberry geranium)	15	7–9	Perennial herb	Partial shade; rock gardens; heavy clay soils	Spreads by runners
Armeria maritima (Thrift)	6	5–9	Perennial herb	Sandy soil; full sun	Small pink flowers in spring
Zebrina pendula (Wandering Jew)	6–9	10	Tender herb	Shade; acid or alkaline soils	Roots easily

Euonymus fortunei (Wintercreeper)	2–4	5–10	Clinging evergreen vine	Sun; shade; ordinary soil	Rapid flat growth; subject to scale insects
Gaultheria procumbens (Wintergreen)	4	5–7	Creeping evergreen	Acid soil; moist shady areas	Creeps over area
Achillea millefolium (Yarrow)	2–3	5–9	Fernlike perennial herb	Adapted to poor dry soil; full sun	Remains green even during drought

CULTIVATED 6
PLANTS
AND FLOWERS

Every plant has its fitness and must be placed in its proper surroundings so as to bring out its full beauty. Therein lies the art of landscaping. When we first understand the character of the individual plant; when we enjoy its development from the time it breaks through the crust of mother earth, sending its first leaves heavenward, until it reaches maturity; when we are willing to give each plant a chance fully to develop its beauty, so as to give us all it possesses without any interference, then, and only then, shall we enjoy ideal landscapes made by man.

Jens Jensen, *Siftings*, 1939

Normally we think of cultivated plants as the annuals, biennials, and perennials that compose flower gradens in traditional landscape designs. However, these plants can also include bushes cultivated for fruit such as raspberries, blackberries, loganberries, currants, gooseberries, and blueberries. Berry patches provide many hours of enjoyable snacks for humans and wild animals alike and are often part of wonderful childhood memories. Some cultivated plants, such as strawberries, can be both ground covers and fruit bearers. Trees, such as apple, pear, cherry, plum, apricot, peach, and nectarine, may already be growing on your land or you may be eager to plant them. What about the long-time garden favorites, the annuals, biennials, and perennials? Do they have a place in the natural landscape?

The answer is both yes and no. Judged solely on whether or not these plants occur in nature where most of us live, the answer has to be no for the overwhelming majority of these plants do not occur in our areas naturally. Instead, they have been transported across state, national, and continental boundaries. And, judged on the basis of how much work they require, the answer in many cases would again be no.

A bed of annuals will require a great deal of your time and effort. You must properly prepare the soil, purchase the plants or raise them from seed, place the plants in the beds, weed, mulch, fertilize, water, and keep a watch out for insects and diseases. Annuals have so many strikes against them that for practical reasons they have very little place in a natural minimum-maintenance landscape. Whether or not you commit yourself to annuals is a decision you will have to make yourself. For a much smaller investment of energy and time, you can prepare a perennial bed for a show of cultivated flowers.

PERENNIALS

Whereas annuals complete their life cycle in a year—germination, growth, flower, seed, and death—and biennials take two years and generally don't flower until the second year, perennials live and flower for at least three years and often longer. Aside from the initial preparation of a perennial flowerbed, perennials require a minimum of maintenance for a maximum return of enjoyment. Once the soil is prepared all you have to do is plant, fertilize occasionally, and water regularly with an oscillating sprinkler. Perennials should be divided every three or more years to keep them growing with plenty of space to spare.

If you choose hardy perennials and prudently stick to those that can withstand winter in your area with little protection, then you don't have to spend time mulching and digging and replanting every year to protect them. Every spring and summer you will be richly rewarded with an ample harvest of flowers that will add color to your garden and around your home.

Before you begin planting perennials, learn as much as possible about them from the books listed in the bibliography, and check with fellow gardeners and members of local garden societies, as well as proprietors of local commercial nurseries. Then decide what your goals are. Do you want to create a formal display garden, organized and planned down to the exact location and number of each type of plant you will use? Or are you simply looking for a place to plant perennials for your own enjoyment? Perhaps you want a place to experiment as a staging ground for plants you may later wish to naturalize and place in the less formal areas of your landscape? Perennials can fit any of these purposes. Their location can be planned on a piece of graph paper. Place the plants according to the amount of space each plant will need—the short plants in front and the tall ones in back. Visualize the total impact of the plants when they begin to grow, flower, and finally die back. Consider the sequence of flowering.

Choose those varieties that stay in flower for the longest periods of time.

You might decide to organize your perennial bed around a variety of flower colors. Or you may wish to make use of a variety of foliage forms and textures. Consider fragrance in your plantings. You may already have fragrant bushes and trees such as magnolias, honeysuckles, and lilacs. Herbs such as mint, basil, lavender, bay, geraniums, lemon verbena, rosemary, thyme, marjoram, savory, chives and sweet woodruff and plants such as sweet violets and lily-of-the-valley are noted for their fragrance.

Planting and Maintenance

Growing perennials successfully requires proper planting. Prepare the soil so that it is adequately watered, has good drainage, and is protected from drying winds. Water enters a well-prepared soil easily. The seeds germinate with few problems. The plants grow strong healthy roots and stems and provide abundant flowers. Better to keep your perennial bed small with well-prepared soil than create a large bed improperly prepared.

To test the soil drainage, dig a hole ten inches deep. Fill it with water. Fill it again the next day and see how long it takes for the water to drain. If it drains in eight to ten hours, you have good drainage. If it takes longer than ten hours, you may have to add sand or additional topsoil to prepare the bed. Spade the soil or use a rototiller to churn the soil to a depth of eight to ten inches. This should be done the first time in the fall. In the spring, several weeks before planting, till the soil again after spreading a layer of compost and fertilizer. Use peat moss if you have no compost. Once the last frost has passed you can plant your seeds or set out the already started plants.

If you buy seed make sure it is fresh, allowing no more than three months between purchase and planting. If you take more time before you plant, the seeds will lose much of their vitality, may fail to germinate, and are likely to produce poor seedlings. Look for F_1 hybrid seeds. They may be more expensive, but their superiority makes up for the additional cost. Store seeds in dry cool places before planting.

Wait until the soil has warmed to about 60° before planting seeds. If you plant the seeds earlier, they will remain dormant in the cool soil and chances are they will rot before having a chance to germinate.

Once you set your seeds or plants out, water them. Use an oscillating sprinkler, not a rotary, to water the plants. Do not water by

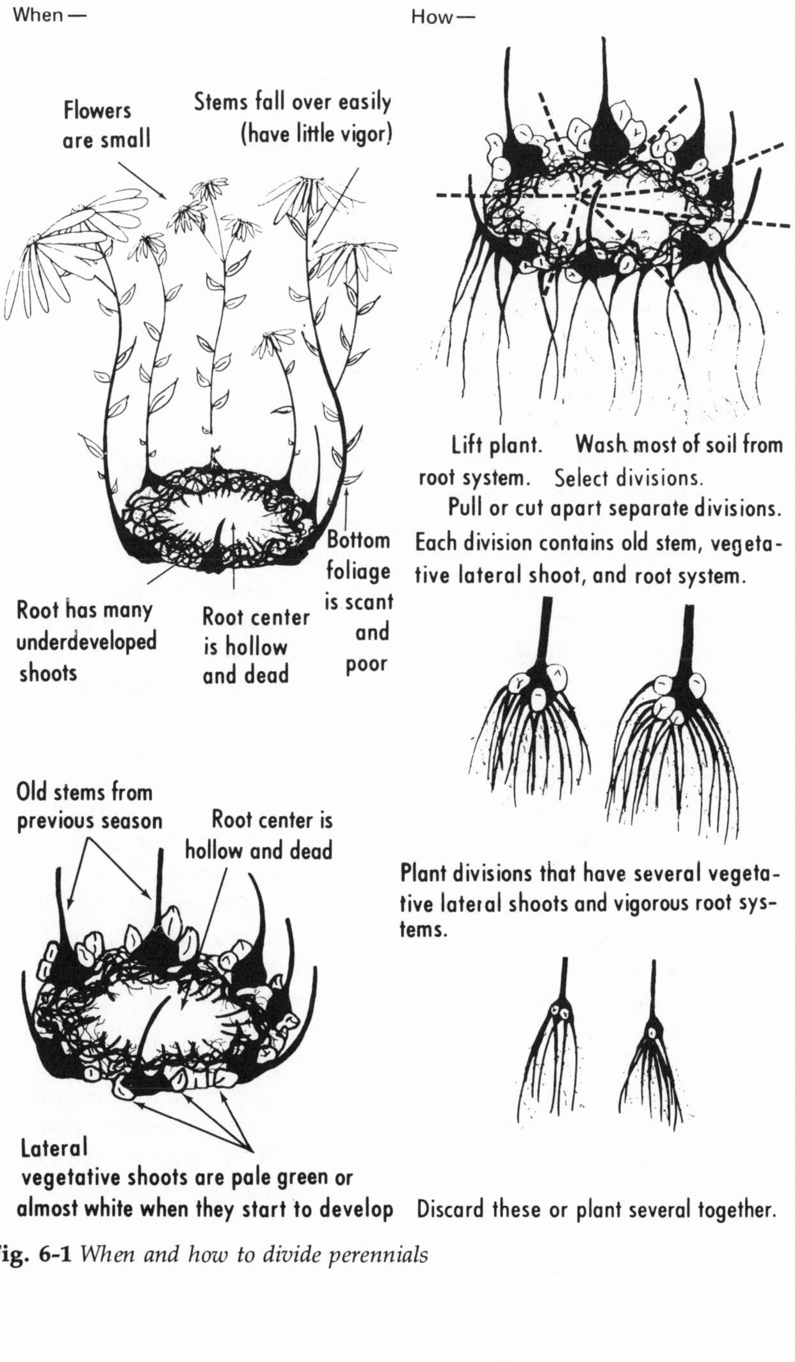

When —

How —

Flowers are small

Stems fall over easily (have little vigor)

Bottom foliage is scant and poor

Root has many underdeveloped shoots

Root center is hollow and dead

Lift plant.   Wash most of soil from root system.   Select divisions.

Pull or cut apart separate divisions. Each division contains old stem, vegetative lateral shoot, and root system.

Old stems from previous season

Root center is hollow and dead

Plant divisions that have several vegetative lateral shoots and vigorous root systems.

Lateral vegetative shoots are pale green or almost white when they start to develop   Discard these or plant several together.

Fig. 6-1 *When and how to divide perennials*

hand. Hand-watering and rotary sprinklers do a poor job because they disturb the surface of the soil and don't water deeply or thoroughly enough. Run the sprinkler at least four hours to get the water down deep into the soil where it will help develop stronger plant roots. Water early in the day so the plants can dry before night. Don't water when the flowers are in bloom. They tend to catch water and rot.

Bulbs are generally planted at a soil depth equal to two and a half times their diameter. Most bulbs will do their best if planted in the early fall. Care must be taken, especially in northern climates, not to plant too late in the fall since any new growth will be damaged before it has a chance to harden before the first frost.

Since most bulbs will remain in their soil for years, it is important that they be planted in good soil with plenty of humus beneath them. That is why it is best to plant them in clumps large enough to allow for good soil preparation. If you are planting them in small groups or individually, use a special bulb-planting spade (it's narrow and long) to dig a deep hole and insert good quality soil in place of poorer earth.

Whether or not to mulch is a personal choice. During the winter the best mulch is snow, as long as the perennial bed has good drainage. During the summer, mulch to hold down weeds, to prevent excessive water evaporation and soil baking and cracking, and to reduce the amount of soil splashing during watering. Of these reasons, the most important is to hold down the weeds. (See Chapter Twelve.) If you have few weeds or don't mind weeding, forget the mulching.

A regular schedule of fertilizing will help keep your perennials at their best since their extensive growing times tend to reduce the soil's natural fertility. Compost or 5-10-5 fertilizer applied two or three times in early spring, at least six weeks apart, will accomplish all that is needed. Some gardeners say they have had success with only one application of compost. (See Chapter Twelve.)

Divide your perennials no more often than every three years. Some perennials require less frequent division. If the plants seem to be increasing in number and you see the foliage getting thinner but the flowers are small, then it is time to divide and open up the amount of space given each plant. The diagrams on page 73 show when and how to divide perennials. Avoid dividing all of your perennials at once. Stagger the work over several years. It will be easier on you and on the plants.

Fig. 6-2 *The anemone pulsatillas can add color to your natural landscape. (Photo by Dean M. Gottehrer)*

Selection of Perennials

The following list of perennials was developed by the U.S. Department of Agriculture. These plants will do well in most areas of the United States, requiring little maintenance, and will winter over fairly easily. Zones refer to the map on page 22. Consult local sources for details specific to your area.

Achillea (Yarrow).   Grows 6 to 24 inches tall. White, pink, or golden flowers that are good for cutting. Grows in moist soil. Space 36 inches apart in sunny area. Seed germinates in 7 to 14 days. Zone 3.

Althaea rosea (Hollyhock).   Grows to 9 feet tall. Use for background. Red, rose, pink, white, or yellow flowers bloom late spring to midsummer. Space plants about 3 feet apart. Seed germinates in about 10 days. Zones 2–3.

Alyssum saxatile (Gold-dust). Grows 9 to 12 inches tall. Use as edging and for cut flowers. Golden blooms in early spring. Does well in dry or sandy soils in sunny spots. Space plants 24 inches apart. Seed germinates in 21 to 28 days. Zone 3.

Anchusa (alkanet).   Grows 4 to 5 feet tall. Use for borders, backgrounds, and cut flowers. Bright blue flowers bloom in June and July. Refrigerate seed for 72 hours before planting in shaded spot. Space 24 inches apart. Seed germinates in 21 to 28 days. Zone 3.

Anemone Pulsatilla (Windflower).   Grows 12 inches tall. Use in borders and pots. Blue to reddish-purple bell-shaped flowers bloom in May and June and are used for cut flowers. Space plants 35 to 42 inches apart. Seed germinates in 4 days. Not hardy north of Washington, D.C. Zone 5.

Anthemis tinctoria (Golden daisy).   Grows about 2 feet tall. Use in borders and for cut flowers, which are aromatic. Various shades of yellow flowers bloom through the summer. Grows well in dry or sandy soil in a sunny spot. Space plants 24 inches apart. Seed germinates in 21 to 28 days. Zone 3.

Arabis alpina (Rock cress).   Grows 8 to 12 inches tall. Use in rock gardens and edging. Small white flowers appear in April–May. Plant in shade, about 12 inches apart. Seed germinates in about 5 days. Zone 3.

Armeria alpina (Sea pink).   Grows 18 to 24 inches tall. Use in borders, edging, and rock gardens. White to deep pink flowers bloom in May and June. Plant in dry sandy soil in sunny spot, 12 inches apart, shaded until plants are sturdy. Seed germinates in about 10 days. Zone 3. Zone 3.

Artemisia stelleriana (Wormwood; dusty miller).   Grows about 2 feet tall. Use in flowerbeds, borders, and rock gardens. Small yellow flowers bloom in late summer. Grows in poor and dry soils. Space 9 to 12 inches apart. Zones 2–3.

Aster alpinus (Hardy aster). Grows 1 to 5 feet tall. Use in rock gardens, borders, and for cut flowers. Violet flowers bloom in May and June. Plant in early spring, in sunny spot, about 3 feet apart. Seed germinates in 14 to 21 days. Zones 2–3.

Astilbe japonica.   Grows 1 to 3 feet tall. Use in borders. Blooms in masses of white clusters in summer. Space 24 inches apart in rich, loamy soil. Seed germinates in 14 to 21 days. Zone 5.

Aubrieta deltoidea graeca (Rainbow rock cress).   Grows about 6 inches tall, in borders, rock gardens, and along dry walls. Red to purple flowers bloom from April to June. Plant about 12 inches apart in light shade. Seed germinates in 20 days. Zone 4.

Begonia evansiana (Hardy begonia).   Grows 12 inches high, in shady areas. Pink flowers bloom in late summer. Space plants 9 to 12 inches apart. Seed germinates in 12 days. Zone 6.

Centaurea montana (Cornflower).   Grows 2 feet tall. Use in borders and for cut flowers. Deep cornflower-blue flowers bloom from June to September. Plant in sunny spot 12 inches apart. Seed germinates in 21 to 28 days. Remove flowers as they fade to prolong blooming. Zones 2–3.

Cerastium tomentosum (Snow-in-summer).   Grows about 6 inches tall. Use in rock gardens and as ground cover. Forms creeping mat that blooms with white flowers May and June. Tough rampant grower that will cover other plants if given a chance. Plant in sunny spot 18 inches apart. Seed germinates in 14 to 24 days. Zones 2–3.

Cheiranthus Cheiri (Siberian wallflower). Grows 12 to 18 inches tall. Use in rock gardens and for cut flowers. Gold, yellow, red, and brown flowers bloom in May and June. Does very well in cool climates. Plant early when soil is still cool, in sunny spot, 1 foot apart. Seed germinates in 5 days. Zone 3.

Crocus.   Grows 4 to 5 inches tall. Use in borders, rock gardens, bare spots, or in front of shrubs. Lilac or white flowers bloom March to April. Plant bulbs 3 inches deep, 3 to 6 inches apart. Can grow in same place for many years. Zone 4.

Delphinium (Larkspur).   Grows between 18 and 60 inches tall. Needs well-drained soil in sunny spot. Blue to purple flowers bloom in June and will rebloom if old flowers are removed. Space plants 24 inches apart. Seed germinates in 20 days. Zones 2–3.

Dianthus barbatus (Sweet William).   Grows 12 to 18 inches tall. Use for borders, edging, and cut flowers. Pink, red or white flowers bloom in May and June. Plant 1 foot apart. Seed germinates in 5 days. Zone 4.

Dianthus deltoides and *D. plumarius* (pinks).   Grows 12 inches tall. Use for borders, edging, cut flowers, and rock gardens. Red, pink, or white flowers bloom in May and June. Plant in sunny spot 12 inches apart. Seed germinates in 5 days. Winterkills in wet locations; tends to rot at soil line. Zones 2–3.

Dicentra (Bleeding heart; Dutchman's breeches). Grows 12 to 48 inches tall. Use for borders, in front of shrubs. Prefers shade. White-to-pink flowers bloom from May until frost. Plant seed in late autumn, 12 to 18 inches apart. Seed germinates in over 50 days. Zones 2–3.

Digitalis purpurea (Foxglove). Grows 4 to 6 feet tall. Use for borders and cut flowers. Purple, drooping, bell-shaped flowers bloom in June and July. Plant in sun or partial shade 12 inches apart. Seed germinates in 20 days. Zone 4.

Gaillardia (Blanket-flower). Grows 12 to 30 inches tall. Use in borders and for cut flowers. Yellow, daisy-like flowers bloom mid-summer to frost. Plant in sunny area 24 inches apart. Seed germinates in 20 days. Zones 2–3.

Gypsophila paniculata (Baby's-breath). Grows 2 to 4 feet tall. Use in borders, for cut flowers, and for drying flowers. Small white clustered flowers bloom from early summer to early autumn. Plant in alkaline soil in sunny spot 4 feet apart. Seed germinates in about 10 days. Zones 2–3.

Helianthemum Nummularium (Sun rose). Grows about 12 inches tall. Use in borders. Evergreen. Yellow, pink, or white flowers bloom June to September. Will grow in dry soil. Plant 12 inches apart. Seed germinates in about 15 days. Zones 5–6.

Hemerocallis (Daylily). Grows 1 to 4 feet tall. Use in borders and among shrubbery. Orange, yellow, or red flowers appear during the spring and summer growing season. Space 24 to 30 inches apart. Propagate from division of clumps to obtain plants that are true to type. Zones 2–3.

Heuchera sanguinea (Coral bells). Grows up to 2 feet tall. Use for rock gardens, borders, and cut flowers. Branched spikes of red-to-pink bell-like flowers bloom from June to September. Plant in alkaline soil in partial shade 18 inches apart. Seed germinates in 10 days. Zone 3.

Hibiscus (Rose mallow). Hybrids grow up to 8 feet tall. White to crimson colorful flowers bloom from July to September. Space plants at least 2 feet apart. Propagate by division of roots. Zone 5.

Iris. Grows from 3 to 30 inches tall. Use in borders and as cut flowers. Purple, red, or brown flowers bloom in spring and early summer.

Fig. 6-3 *A primula veris in bloom (Photo by Dean M. Gottehrer)*

Plant bulbs or rhizomes in late fall for germination the following spring. Space 18 to 24 inches apart. Zone 3.

Lathyrus latifolius (Everlasting sweet pea).   Grows 5 to 6 feet tall. Use as a background vine on a fence or trellis and for cut flowers. Rose-colored flowers bloom June to September. Succeeds almost without care anywhere. Plant about 2 feet apart. Seed germinates in 20 days. Zone 3.

Liatris pycnostachya (Gay-feather).   Grows 2 to 6 feet tall. Use in borders and for cut flowers. Purple flowers bloom summer to early autumn. Plant seed in sunny spot 18 inches apart. Seed germinates in 20 days. Zone 3.

Limonium latifolium (Sea lavender).   Grows 2 to 3 feet tall. Use for bedding, cut flowers, and flowers for drying. Bright mauve flowers bloom in July and August. Plant in early spring when soil is cool, in sunny spot, 30 inches apart. Seed germinates in 15 days. Zone 3.

Fig. 6-4 *The lily-of-the-valley adds color and fragrance to your landscape. Bring it inside the house to add its aroma to your home. (Photo by Dean M. Gottehrer)*

Linum perenne (Flax).   Grows about 2 feet tall. Use in bedding and rock gardens. Deep blue flowers bloom much of the summer. Space 18 inches apart. Seed germinates in 25 days. Zone 4.

Lunaria biennis (Money plant).   Grows about 4 feet tall. Use in a cutting garden and as a source of seedpods for drying in bouquets. White and purple flowers bloom in summer. Space plants 2 feet apart. Seed germinates in 10 days. Zone 4.

Lythrum (Blackblood).   Grows 4 to 6 feet tall. Scatter in gardens and among trees and shrubs. Deep rose to red-purple flowers bloom July and August. Plant in moist, lightly shaded areas 18 to 24 inches apart. Seed germinates in 15 days. Zone 3.

Monarda (Bee balm; horse mint).   Grows to 2 to 3 feet tall. Use in borders and for masses of scarlet, yellow or purple. Blooms all summer. Cut back after first bloom, will flower again same season. Plant 12 to 18 inches apart. Seed germinates in 15 days. Zone 4.

Fig. 6-5 *Phlox subulata makes an excellent and colorful ground cover. (Photo by Dean M. Gottehrer)*

Narcissus (Daffodil).   Grows 3 to 20 inches tall. Use for flowers. White and yellow flowers bloom March to June. Plant bulbs 4 to 6 inches deep, 4 to 8 inches apart in September and October. Zone 4.

Paeonia (Peony).   Grows 2 to 4 feet tall. Use in borders and for cut flowers. Light pink to deep red or white flowers bloom late spring and early summer. Difficult to grow from seed. Plant tubers in late fall and at least 3 feet apart, 2 to 3 inches deep. Zone 3.

Papaver nudicaule (Iceland poppy); *P. orientale* (Oriental poppy). Grows 15 to 18 inches tall in the Iceland poppy and 3 feet tall in the Oriental poppy. Yellow, green, orange, pink, and red flowers in the Iceland, and white through pink to red in the Oriental bloom in May and June. Both are used in borders and for cut flowers. Plant in a sunny place in a permanent location (they do not transplant well), 2 feet apart. Seed germinates in about 10 days. Zone 2.

Pentstemon murrayanus grandiflorus (Beardlip; pagoda flower).   Grows 18 to 24 inches tall. Use in borders and for cut flowers. Planted early,

Fig. 6-6 *The iris flower is also used for cutting. (Photo by Dean M. Gottehrer)*

scarlet flowers bloom through the summer. Plant in well-drained dry soil, 18 inches apart. Seed germinates in about 10 days. Zone 6.

Phlox paniculata (Summer phlox).   Grows about 3 feet tall. Use in borders and for cut flowers. Red, pink, purple or white flowers bloom early summer. Refrigerate seed for 1 month before planting. Space plants 2 feet apart. Keep soil moist. Seed germination irregular, takes about 25 days. Zone 4.

Primula (Primrose).   Grows 6 to 9 inches tall. Use in rock gardens, edging, and along a stream. With a variety of different colors, the flowers bloom in April and May. Plant in rich well-drained soil in shaded spot, about 1 foot apart. Seed germinates in 25 days, but very irregularly. Zones 2–3.

Pyrethrum roseum (Chrysanthemum; painted daisy).   Grows about 2 feet tall. Use in borders and for cut flowers. White through pink to red flowers bloom in May and June. Plant in sunny well-drained soil, about 18 inches apart. Seed germinates in 20 days. Zones 2–3.

Fig. 6-7 *One of the many species of cultivated lily (Photo by Dean M. Gottehrer)*

Salvia azurea grandiflora (Blue Sage).   Grows 3 to 4 feet tall. Use in borders. Blue flowers bloom from August to frost. Plant 18 to 24 inches apart. Seed germinates in 15 days. Zone 4.

Stokesia cyanea (Stokes aster).   Grows 15 inches tall. Use for borders and cut flowers. Blue to purplish-blue flowers bloom from July to October. Plant 18 inches apart. Seed germinates in about 20 days. Zone 5.

Trollius ledebouri (Globeflower).   Grows about 20 inches tall. Use in borders. Yellow flowers bloom May to July. Requires extra moisture. Place seed outdoors over winter for germination. To plant seed in early spring, soak it in hot water for 30 minutes before sowing. Plant 1 foot apart. Seed germinates in over 50 days. Zone 3.

Tulipa (Tulip).   Grows 3 to 40 inches tall according to variety. Use for landscaping and cut flowers. Flowers in almost all colors but true blue bloom early to late spring. Bulbs planted 4 to 6 inches deep late October, early November. Bulbs should be replaced when flowers get smaller, after approximately 3 years. Zone 4.

Veronica spicata (Speedwell).   Grows 18 inches tall. Use in borders and rock gardens and for cut flowers. Blue or pink flowers bloom in June and July. Easily grown. Plant in sunny spot 18 inches apart. Seed germinates in about 15 days. Zone 3.

Viola Cornuta (Tufted pansy).   Grows about 6 inches tall. Use for bedding, edging, and window boxes. Purple and apricot flowers bloom all summer if old flowers are removed. Plant in partial shade, about 1 foot apart. Seed germinates in 10 days. Zone 6.

WATER 7

The rippling murmer of a stream cascading down over rocks, the placid stillness of a pond, the gentle sway of a water lily as a goldfish swims by—these are the aesthetic pleasures of having water in the natural landscape. Aside from providing beauty, and maintaining vegetation growth, water performs other functions as well. You should consider adding it to your natural landscape if it does not already exist there.

PONDS

Natural ponds have been used in landscape design for many different reasons. The pond surface, a flat horizontal line, provides contrast to vertical elements such as trees. In this sense, the pond anchors the elements of the landscape design. The surface of a pond is a mirror, which adds to, as it reflects, the natural beauty. The rocks of the shoreline can form an integral part of the landscape design if they are prominent enough. Finally, the plant life surrounding a pond can be an interesting contrast to the vegetation in drier areas.

Changing a pond. It may be necessary to change the water level of a natural pond. Such changes may make the pond usable for swimming, increase the amount of water stored in the pond, change the local climate, make the water in the pond cooler, spread the pond over a greater area to benefit local wildlife, and visually modify the landscape.

Many states have laws that govern water use and the design and construction of ponds. Before taking any action to change a pool, pond, or stream, determine what the local regulations or state laws have to say about what you contemplate doing.

There are two ways to increase the depth of a pond. You can raise the water level by damming the outlets or you can deepen the pond by dredging the bottom. If you decide to dam the water outlets, you will need one or more spillways, preferably with adjustable gates, to manipulate the depth of the pond.

Decreasing the depth of the pond is one way to decrease the mosquito population. As you lower the pond's water level, you expose mosquito larvae to the air and sun. This will kill them and reduce the number of mosquitoes. But frequently manipulating the water level in a pond prevents the vegetation and animal wildlife from following their normal path of growth and development. If you want a natural development of the local plants and animals, you will have to choose another method of controlling the mosquitoes that breed in the pond's water.

If it is not practical to drain the pond to deepen it, you can use a dragline to dredge the bottom. If you can drain the water, you can hire a bulldozer and dredge the bottom when it is dry in any way you care to, subject to local law.

As long as your pond isn't inhabited by fish, you may consider another method—the use of dynamite. In the hands of a professional who knows what needs to be done, dynamite can be an exacting excavator. However, if you deepen a pond this way you may lose the pond. It is possible that there may be underneath the soil at the bottom of your pond an impervious layer of rock. If that layer of rock extends down quite a distance from the bottom of the pond, there is no problem using the dynamite to deepen the pond. If the impervious layer simply covers a permeable layer of rock, however, then the dynamite may blast through the impervious layer. This would open up the bottom of the pond to the permeable rock and cause the pond to empty like a bathtub with its drain plug pulled.

As you consider other alterations you may wish to make to your natural pond, one thought to keep in mind is that an irregular shoreline with a variety of water depths will provide the proper environment for a variety of different kinds of plants for animal food and cover.

Creating a pond.   If you do not have a pond on your property already you may be able to create one. Look for the best spot. A clump of shrubs or ferns makes a good backdrop for a pond. While willows and maples appreciate having a pond nearby, pines and hemlocks do not benefit from having their roots constantly dampened by the pond. Consider the area that the pond will reflect and where you can best obtain an irregular shoreline. In addition to the visual considerations,

Fig. 7-1 *Out from among the pads, the water lilly blossom adds beauty to the natural waterscape. (Photo by Dean M. Gottehrer)*

you must also assess the type of soil and rock in the area to determine whether it will hold water. Clay, silty clay, and some sandy clays will hold water for a pond. Sand, gravel, and sand-gravel combinations are poor candidates for pond bottoms.

If you do put your pond in an area that later develops more seepage than you find desirable, you may be able to solve the problem by using a sealant to reduce the seepage. Chemical dispersants, which are similar to some detergents, will run the soil particles together to prevent the water from seeping out. Expansive clays, such as betonite, will expand and fill in the spaces in the soil to hold the water in place. And if it is possible to place flexible plastic or rubber over the bottom, these impermeable materials will also prevent excess seepage.

The two most common methods of creating a pond both first require that nature be on your side and provide the water. You can either dam up a stream, providing the law allows it, or, lacking a stream, you can dig the pond. You must, however, have a water table that is high enough to fill up the hole you dig. Otherwise you will

Fig. 7-2 *A waterfall into a lake can be a place of serenity and peace in your natural landscape. (Photo by Dean M. Gottehrer)*

have an unsightly hole instead of a water-filled pond. Find a place where you can dig down a few feet and reach the water table. Then dig down the desired depth of your pond below the water level.

Before you dam a stream, consider the effects of your action. How big will the pond be? What effect will it have on the surrounding land? Will it cause or prevent erosion? What effect will it have on plant and animal life? Will the pond be more valuable than the stream was? Will the pond remove vegetation that feeds local animals? What will happen downstream from the pond? How will the pond affect boating, swimming, fishing, and other stream-related activities?

Fig. 7-3 *Ducks may naturally be attracted to your water areas if you provide the proper food for them. (Photo by Dean M. Gottehrer)*

Do any necessary grading before you dam off the stream. You may want to create a harbor for canoes and boats, a beach for swimming (you can truck in the sand much easier before the stream is dammed off than later), and you may also want to build boat-launching ramps.

To construct a dam, you must examine the soil you plan to use. Will it prove resistant to erosion? Can you provide an emergency spillway to prevent the pressure from building up to too great a level on the dam and taking it out? A dam should be at least 10 to 12 feet wide at the top to be adequate for the average small pond. The sides should slope down at a rate of one foot of vertical drop for every three feet horizontally.

In any pond you build, be sure to have a rock island in the middle of the pond, surrounded by water. This will be a good resting place for frogs, turtles, ducks and salamanders. In return for your generosity, these animals will consume insects and control the pest population around your pond.

For additional information on constructing ponds, consult the U.S. Department of Agriculture, Soil Conservation Service (12th St.

and Independence, S.W., Washington DC 20250); Sports Fishing Institute (608 13th. St., N.W., Washington, DC 20005); Wildlife Management Institute (709 Wire Bldg., Washington, DC 20005); Izaak Walton League (800 N. Kent St., Suite 806, Arlington, VA 22209); and/or the National Audubon Society (950 Third Ave., New York, NY 10022).

STREAMS AND CREEKS

Remember the stream or creek of your childhood where you tossed rocks in the water to see the ripples and listened to the different sounds the water made? If you treasure these experiences you will realize that the best thing to do with a stream is to leave it alone. The natural stream may not provide all that a dammed-up stream will in the way of water storage, flood and drought control, and all the rest, but it will supply years of enjoyment, mystery, and beauty.

Still, there are a few things you can legitimately consider in altering the nature of a stream. First, you can clean it up. There aren't many streams left these days that haven't been defiled by garbage and litter in and around the streambed. You may also have natural waste—tree branches, leaves, and so forth—that you will want to remove to improve the view.

You may want to experiment with changing the sound of a stream. Listen to the sound as the product of a concert orchestra. Each rock, pebble, or boulder is an instrument in the orchestra. If you move the rocks, pebbles, and boulders around, remove some and add others, or place boards in the stream, you will change the music the stream composes. Make changes slowly, a few at a time, so that you can restore the original flow should you so desire.

You should also be aware of the effects of making a stream deeper or shallower. Deepening a stream will cool the water, speed up the current, and increase the water's oxygen content. Making the stream shallower will have the opposite effect. Both of these actions will affect the animal and plant life living in or near the stream.

POOLS

If you have no stream or pond, there is only one recourse left—build a pool. It is somewhat difficult to make a constructed pool appear like a natural pond, especially if there is no water flowing through your property. Without flowing water, your pool will be much smaller than a stream-fed pond or an excavated pond.

No pool, especially one in which you plan to have plants and fish, should have a depth less than 15 inches. The depth of the pool is usually determined by the surface area of the water. A pool 100 square feet should be 18 inches deep. Between 100 and 300 square feet, a pool should be 24 inches deep. Between 300 and 1,000 square feet, a pool should have a depth of 30 inches. Over 1,000 square feet, there is no need to increase the pool's depth.

Before you construct a pool, lay it out on the ground so you can appreciate its three-dimensional impact. You will probably want to make changes in your design, or you may find that you don't want a pool after all.

When you construct the pool, slope the sides 20° from vertical. You can also include a shelf that is 9 inches below water level on which you can place marginal plants that do not require the same depth in the water as water lilies, for example. Avoid placing the pool in the shade or near trees and shrubs that will shed their leaves into the pool and cause maintenance problems. If it is impossible to place the pool in a sunny area, then it should be in the shade no longer than half a day.

If your main interest in a pool is the plants, realize that each water lily should have at least 15 square feet of water surface. Mosquitoes in the pool can be controlled either by frequently draining the pool or by using fish that will eat the mosquito larvae.

FISH

You may want to stock your pond with game fish. Some states have programs for stocking fish in ponds. The department of wildlife and fisheries in your state may be helpful in providing or selling spawns with which to stock your pond. Be sure not to overstock your pond or pool. Each fish one or more inches long should have one gallon of water. (Measure the cubic feet of the pool and multiply by 7.48 to find the number of gallons in the pool.) Fish will begin to die off in an overstocked pond or pool.

Pool fish should not be of the same species as those in ponds. Many varieties of goldfish and other exotics and natives can be stocked in a pool that will keep it clean and free of mosquito larvae and will add another dimension to the beauty of the pool.

Snails and clams are useful animals to have in ponds and pools. They scavenge off rotting vegetation and help keep the pool clean.

Remember that when you are stocking a pool with plants and fish, put the plants in first. Wait at least a few weeks before putting in any fish. Fish will nibble at the plants. This does the plants no harm as long as they are firmly rooted. Give the plants a chance to root and establish themselves sturdily in the soil.

WATER PLANTS

Plants can be added to ponds as well as pools. A pond, however, will require fewer plants since it will naturally contain many plants adapted to water culture. In fact ponds may have problems due to a proliferation of plants rather than a shortage.

What is most necessary to a pool or a pond that is used for growing fish is a good supply of submerged oxygenators. These plants absorb carbon dioxide from the water, use the carbon for their own growth, and return the oxygen back into the water. Submerged oxygenators are often called water weeds because they multiply so fast and often have to be kept in check. They also provide welcome shelter for young fish scurrying away from their cannabalistic elders and probably were the home from which the youngsters spawned. You should have approximately one plant for every square foot of water.

Deep-water Plants

Aquatic plants are divided according to the depth of the water they appreciate—deep, marginal, and floating. Among the deep-water aquatic plants, the most widely used and appreciated are the water lilies. Water lilies are of two types—tropical and hardy. The natural landscaper in northern climates will probably shun the tropical lilies that require protection during the winter to prevent them from freezing. The hardy water lilies will be more attractive, since they can usually pass through the winter safely, protected only by the ice on top of the pond or pool, providing the water depth is at least ten inches. (To prevent pools from cracking in the winter, toss in an old log before the surface freezes.)

Water lilies require very little attention to get them growing and flowering abundantly. They need only be planted at the correct depth (which varies from 3 to 36 inches, depending on the variety), in reasonably warm water away from any cold-water springs and stiff cur-

Fig. 7-4 *A man-made waterfall can accent an alpine or rock garden. (Photo by Dean M. Gottehrer)*

rents. Water lilies are usually planted on the bottom of a pond. Leaving them in the container from the nursery makes it easier to take the water lilies out of the pond and rearrange them. Most lilies, except for the miniatures, will grow in a depth of 10 to 12 inches of water above the soil and plant crown. Lilies that will tolerate greater depths can also be grown in shallower water. The more sun the plants get the more they will bloom. Finally, in the fall, after the frosts set in, the lily growth will disappear. In the spring, new growth will appear and the perennial cycle will continue.

Marginal Plants

Marginal plants grow with their roots in shallow water and their stems, foliage, and flowers above the water line. Marginal plants are not important to the life of the pool—they do not contribute to the water's chemistry by adding oxygen, nor do they clear the water or provide shade for the fish. They are chosen primarily for the ornamental value of their leaves and flowers. Marginals are planted on the pool shelf in a six-inch-deep container, which when placed on the nine-inch-deep shelf provides a distance of three inches from the surface of the water to the top of the container. This water depth suits the majority of marginals.

Floating Plants

Floating aquatic plants have only one thing in common. They don't plant their roots in the soil at the pond or pool bottom. Some are hardy and can pass through the winter; others need protection. Some are valued for their ornamental use alone. Others perform a useful function in the pool; for example, forming a carpet of tiny plants. These plants float on the surface and reduce the amount of sunlight entering. This discourages the growth of algae.

The following is a list of aquatic plants, including bog and marsh plants, that are hardy. No plant has been included on the list, except where noted, that must be removed from or protected in a pool or pond to pass safely through the winter.

Acorus Calamus (Sweet flag).   A hardy perennial, native to the northern hemisphere. Grows in marginal and bog areas, with leaves that reach three feet in length, and bears yellowish flowers in the summer.

Alisma (Water plantain).   A hardy and strong reproducing aquatic plant that grows in still waters, near the edge, to a height of two to three feet. Produces small white flowers in the summer. Control the free-seeding habits by removing the dead flowers before the seeds have a chance to spread.

Anacharis (Elodea).   Also known as water thyme, a submerged aquatic valued for its use as an oxygenator. Has dark green, spiked foliage that remains that way through the winter. Tends to grow uncontrolled and can become a pest. Yellowed foliage should be removed. Controls algae growth.

Azolla caroliniana (Fairy moss).   A floating fern of mossy green forms a carpet in the water. Dies back every winter, to be reborn from spore. Hardy in all but the most severe winters. Not recommended for small pools or ponds because it may spread rapidly and become a nuisance.

Calla palustris.   A hardy plant that grows at the water's edge. Produces heart-shaped and arum-type flowers that are green, white and yellow, followed by clusters of red berries in the autumn.

Caltha (Marsh marigold). A hardy marsh or bog plant. The various species grow from nine inches to three feet tall and all flower early in the spring. Flowers are yellow or white tinted with blue. Produces heart-shaped leaves.

Ceratophyllum demersum (Hornwort). A hardy oxygenator, with submerged bristle-like leaves that will grow in deep water. May grow to between one and two feet long. Thrives in most situations including cold or shaded pools and ponds.

Iris. A genus of hardy bulb or tuber-rooted perennials that are native to northern areas of the country. Come in many different species, colors, and shapes. Consult your local nurseryman to select those most appropriate to your area.

Lemna (Duckweed). A hardy perennial that floats on the surface and provides food for the fish, although they may not keep its rapid growth in check.

Lobelia. A genus of some 200 species of annuals and perennials that grow all over the tropical and sub-tropical parts of the world. Many are not hardy. One that is and provides beautiful scarlet-crimson flowers that appear from July to September is *L. cardinalis* (Cardinal flower). Grows in marginal waters or in marshes.

Lythrum Salicaria (Purple loosestrife). Grows in marginal pond waters. Has reddish-purple, spike-shaped flowers that bloom during the summer.

Menyanthes trifoliata (Bogbean). A hardy marsh plant or a shallow water marginal. Produces unusual white and pink flowers in the summer that have fine upright fringe attached to the petals.

Mimulus. A genus of annuals and perennials, only some of which are hardy enough to survive through the winter. Most grow in shallow water or wet soil and have been found native to temperate parts of North America.

Nymphaea (Water lily). Comes in a wide assortment of colors and degrees of hardiness. Be sure any you purchase are hardy enough to survive your winters. Even the hardy water lilies die back in the fall, to grow again in the spring and bring forth their lovely flowers. Worth the effort to find hardy varieties.

Onoclea sensibilis (Sensitive fern). A fern that likes the moist edge of a marsh or pond. Grows four half-foot fronds.

Orontium aquaticum (Golden club). Its common name comes from the two-inch-long spikes covered with yellow flowers that appear in early summer. Will grow to any depth of water from marshside to 18 inches.

Pontederia cordata (Pickerel plant). A hardy aquatic that grows in marginal water about 12 inches deep. Produces beautiful blue aquatic flowers that bloom throughout the summer. The heart-shaped leaves point skyward and the plant reaches a height of 18 to 24 inches.

Sagittaria (Arrowhead). Has 20 species of hardy aquatic perennials with arrow-shaped leaves. There are a few tender tropical species. Flourishes in marginal water areas, five to six inches deep. Have decorative white summer flowers. Also performs valuable oxygenating and water-cleansing functions with their underwater leaves.

Typha (Cat-tail). A large hardy plant that grows to eight feet and is thus most appropriate in large bodies of water. The brownish-black flower spikes turn to billowy fluff that floats away and reseeds the plant for the next year.

WILDFLOWERS 8

Who among us has not walked in the still untamed areas of the country—along the beaches, through the forests, across the prairies, and into the deserts—and not come away with a respect for the beauties of nature in the wild? A child may be fascinated by a Jack-in-the-pulpit, which looks like a little person shaded by a hood. The adolescent may be enthralled by the blooms on a desert cactus. And the adult recalls with pleasure the natural wild beauty of plants known in childhood.

In every area of the country there are wildflower species that are rare or endangered. Lists of these wild plants can be obtained from local and state environmental protection agencies and wildlife and conservation organizations. If you choose to conserve these endangered plants, take the time and care to learn what the laws are governing collection of wildflowers. You can use your natural landscape as a wildflower preserve. Scout out local areas marked for development, of which there seems to be a never-ending supply, and search there for endangered or rare species of wildflowers and other wild plants that might be eradicated if you don't intervene. It is possible that you may be able to prevent destruction of delicate and rare plants by preventing the development of the land on which they are found. If you are unsuccessful in preventing "progress," you should be allowed to attempt to save whatever you can from the land. This chapter will provide some hints on what you can do to increase your chances of successfully replanting specimens collected from development and other sites.

Protection and conservation may not be your motivation. You may want a wildflower garden to enjoy for its own sake, for the beauty the flowers present, and for the natural aspect they will contribute to your landscape. Even with this purpose in mind you should be careful to know what the local and state laws are governing wild

Fig. 8-1 *The Jack-in-the-pulpit is so unusually shaped that it often fascinates children. (Photo by Dean M. Gottehrer)*

Fig. 8-2 *A wild desert flower (Photo by Dean M. Gottehrer)*

Fig. 8-3 *A trillium in bloom (Photo by Dean M. Gottehrer)*

plants. If you decide to collect your specimens from local areas, you must know whether or not there are certain plants you cannot collect, how to get permission to collect plants, and what, if any, areas of the locale are protected from collecting. In some states you must obtain permission from the landowner in writing before you can collect any plants. Even if that is not required, you should at least protect yourself by talking with the landowner and securing verbal permission to collect plants on his or her property.

You may want to include wild plants for their food value to the animals, rather than for their aesthetic contribution. Rabbits and woodchucks like to eat the blossoms and new spring growth from many plants. Slugs eat the seedlings and blossoms of many plants. Ants will eat arbutus seeds. Deer will munch on orchids, trilliums, and other delicious plants. If you wish to protect the plants from animals, fence in the area or protect each plant individually.

STARTING WILDFLOWERS IN THE NATURAL LANDSCAPE

Start to think about wildflowers early in the design of your natural landscape, although you won't be planting them until later on. It is absolutely crucial, for the plant to grow and prosper, that the wildflower habitat duplicate almost exactly the conditions from which a plant comes. To accomplish this there are two ways to introduce wildflowers into the landscape. You can collect plants from any type of environment and attempt to recreate that environment on your home grounds. Or you can plant only those wildflowers that are native to the area and that will have no trouble surviving in the natural landscape as it exists. If any modifications are needed, they should be minor ones. The natural landscaper usually prefers native plants because they require far less work and promise far greater success. Both approaches, however, require study and thought.

Some wildflowers, transplanted from one area to another, appear to grow normally for a few years. Then all of a sudden the plant dies back never to appear again. What seemed to work wasn't really working at all. It simply took time for the error to become apparent. Other plants will fail more immediately. If you want all of your wildflowers to succeed, study closely their natural habitat in terms of soil quality, air moisture, light, and shade. The closer you come to duplicating it, the greater your chances for success. Before you move any wild plant, you should know all about its growing pattern and how it sends out its roots (shallow or deep, long or short, fragile or sturdy).

Some plants—pink lady's-slipper, for example—are easily transported and transplanted. Others are virtually impossible to move. For example, most of the orchids are extremely difficult to move. It would be foolhardy for any but the most experienced wildflower gardener to try.

There are reasons, after all, why wildflowers are still wild and not cultivated. The main reason is that they are not as hardy as cultivated plants and will not grow under as wide a variety of conditions. This is not to say that growing wildflowers is impossible, but you should realize that there are difficulties. You must know what you are doing before you do it, so no damage is done to what may be a rare and endangered species.

The factors to be examined in selecting wildflowers for your natural landscape include soil, climate, terrain, moisture, sunlight, surrounding ground cover, and other associated plants. It is important to know what combination of these factors is most favorable for the plants you are contemplating for your natural landscape. The correct amount of sunlight or shade, an adequate supply of moisture (if you don't want to be watering all summer long), a winter that is not

Fig. 8-4 *Lady's-slipper*

Fig. 8-5 *Mountain laurel grows wild. (Photo by Dean M. Gottehrer)*

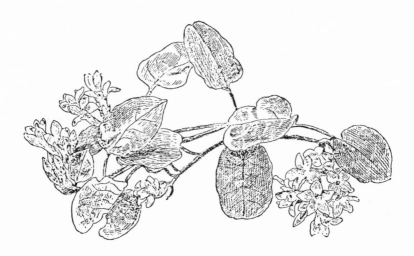

Fig. 8-6 *Trailing arbutus*

Fig. 8-7 *Hepatica*

going to kill the plants, a terrain that provides the right amount of slope or flatness—all of these are important to successful growing of wildflowers. And once established, a successful wildflower garden needs very little or no maintenance to perpetuate itself.

Soil. The most important consideration in successfully growing wildflowers is the soil; in particular, the plant's need for or abhorence of acid in the soil. Some wild plants that love acid soil include wild azaleas, mountain laurel, pink lady's-slipper, trailing arbutus, hepaticas, blueberries, star grass and wood anemones. Some plants, such as wild geraniums, will tolerate varying degrees of soil acidity.

Most wildflowers, however, prefer a soil that is neutral to slightly acidic. If the wild plants are purchased commercially, the nursery can describe the acidity the plants need. If you are going to collect a plant from a nearby locale, you can check the pH of the soil there before moving the plant. If poison ivy or goldenrod grow in the soil, you can be sure that it contains little or no acidity.

The scientifically oriented natural landscaper will test the acidity of the ground's soil before planting. Soil pH is easily determined with litmus paper, which tests for acidity or alkalinity. Soil testing kits are available at nurseries or from mail order seed or nursery catalogues. You may want to send a sample of the soil to the soil-testing lab at your state agricultural extension service—see the section on improving the soil in Chapter Twelve. Once the acidity is determined, the landscaper knows whether or not the soil meets the requirements of the plants. If the soil does not, it is probably not worth the tremendous effort required to change the soil's pH. The reason is that over a period of time the soil will tend to revert to its natural pH. Then the landscaper is left with the choice of whether to allow the plant to suffer or die as a result or change the soil once more to reach the pH the plant needs. In either event, the outcome is not a desirable one. Rather, the landscaper should change to plants that will more closely match the degree of acidity naturally found in the soil. It is a much simpler solution.

You can get a hint of soil's acidity by looking at the vegetation and rock formations in the area. The presence of granite tends to make a soil acid. The presence of limestone will make it alkaline. Coniferous trees tend to create acidic soils because their leaves are acidic. The same is true of oak, beech, rhododendrons, azaleas, laurels, and hemlocks. On the other hand, maples, poplars, hickory, ash, cedar, and basswood trees tend to create a soil that is only slightly acid. As you come to know the acid tolerances of various wildflowers and other wild plants you will be able to determine the preferences of a new plant simply by recognizing its neighbors whose preferences you already know.

Selecting wildflowers. One of the best ways to find the plants you want to have in your natural landscape is to visit areas around you where wildflowers are growing. See what grows there. Note the growing conditions throughout the year. Then, if the area is similar to yours, you can be fairly certain that those plants will grow in your natural landscape.

Fig. 8-8 *Anemone (Photo by Dean M. Gottehrer)*

Consult the books listed in the bibliography. You should know, however, that no book will tell the whole story about a wild plant, the circumstances under which it will or will not grow, or provide enough information to allow you to be certain that you are not making a mistake. Despite all the thinking and investigating that you will do before you plant wildflowers, you may still find that you have to depend on trial and error.

Some wildflowers can be selected by the home landscaper to solve problems posed by areas of the home grounds that may be too wet, too muddy, too dry, too sandy, and so forth. Often there will be wildflowers that will thrive under just those problem conditions. For example, sunflowers can cover the fact that water collects under the drainspout. They thrive there because of the dampness.

Planting wildflowers. Planting wildflowers is not the same as planting a bed of perennials. First, wildflowers will not thrive in an area where all of the ground cover has been cleared. As we noted earlier, it is a mistake to remove all of the vegetation around a new house. That vegetation gives you an idea about the acidity of your soil and what grew there previously. You would know what wildflowers would be expected to grow there successfully now. Always put wildflowers in

Fig. 8-9 *Sunflowers thrive easily and provide food for birds and other animals as well. (Photo by Dean M. Gottehrer)*

an area where they have other plants and ground cover around them. Some wildflowers need, in addition, tree shade to generate their growth. Bare ground will harm these plants.

A good covering of organic matter will help the plants by holding moisture, aerating the soil, and serving as a natural mulch. Here again you can see the advantage of the falling leaves of deciduous trees, especially in areas where you need to preserve the soil's pH. It also helps to have organic matter in the soil to provide food for the bacteria that in turn provides food for the plants. You can also work leaf mold or organic compost into your soil. You must balance the additional work these natural foods will require of you against the benefits they will bring your plants.

If you are planning on planting wildflowers in shade and sandy or dry soil, be sure that either the plants are recommended for that or you have found them growing under those circumstances. Otherwise you will have to water the so-called wild plants all summer long to insure their long life.

Don't begin your garden with seed. Seed for wildflowers can be very difficult to germinate. The procedures, detailed in some of the books listed in the bibliography, can be complicated, time-consuming, and can yield unsatisfying results. After you have established some wildflowers in your natural landscape, you may decide you want to experiment with growing from seed, but it is best to begin with established plants.

Obtaining wildflower plants. You can collect specimens yourself, making certain that you are not collecting endangered species and that you have the permission of the property owner. You can also buy wild plants from nurseries. Choose a local nursery that can tell you about the plant's growing habits and needs and that will be more likely to provide plants hardy for your area. If a nursery or a mail order house advises you that a plant is difficult to grow, you should respect the fact that the dealer is not trying to sell you an exotic plant that has little or no chance of succeeding. The following is a list of nurseries and mail order suppliers who specialize in wildflowers, ferns, perennials, and other native American plants. No recommendation is implied by inclusion. Any omissions are not intended. All are listed in alphabetical order by state.

Clyde Robin Seed Co., Box 2091, Castro Valley, CA 94546. Wildflowers, wild trees, seeds, and plants. Catalogue $1.

The Shop in the Sierra, Box 1, Midpines, CA 95345. Native western plants. Catalogue $1.

J. L. Hudson, Seedsman, Box 1058, Redwood City, CA 94064. Wildflower seeds.

Theodore Payne Foundation for Wild Flowers and Native Plants, 10459 Tuxford St., Sun Valley, CA 91352. California wildflower seeds.

Applewood Seed Co., 833 Parfet St., Lakewood, CO 80215. Western wildflower seeds.

Ruth Hardy's Wildflower and Fern Nursery, Route 7, South Canaan Road, Falls Village, CT 06031. Wildflowers and ferns.

S. D. Coleman Nurseries, Highway 37, Fort Gaines, GA 31751. Nursery-grown native azaleas, rhododendrons, and ferns.

Lounsberry Garden, Box 135, Oakford, IL 62673. Wildflowers, ferns, perennials, and rock garden plants.

Midwest Wildflowers, Box 64, Rockton, IL 61072. Seeds of mid-western native plants.

Conley's Garden Center, Boothbay, ME 04538. Wildflowers, ferns, native ground covers, and vines.

Thoreau Wildgarden, Myra Road, Greenfield, ME 04423. Wildflowers and ferns.

Blackthorne Gardens, 48 Quincy St., Holbrook, MA 02343. Wildflowers, ferns, lilies, and other bulbs.

Arthur Eames Allgrove, 281 Woburn St., North Wilmington, MA 01887. Wildflowers, ferns, and terrarium plants.

Dutch Mountain Nursery, Augusta, MI 49012. Wildflowers, trees, shrubs, and vines for conservation and feeding wild animals.

Rakestraw's Perennial Gardens, G-3094 S. Term St., Burton, MI 48529. Rock garden plants, perennials, and wild dwarf conifers.

Ferndale Nursery and Greenhouse, Askov, MN 55704. Wildflowers and ferns. In business since 1906.

Orchid Gardens, Route 1, Box 245, Grand Rapids, MN 55744. Wildflowers, ferns, shrubs, and perennials. Catalogue $.35, price list free.

Hi-Mountain Farm, Seligman, MO 65745. Wildflowers and ferns.

Radford H. Palmer, RFD 1, Durham, NH 03824. Wildflowers, ferns, bulbs, and aquatic plants.

Charles H. Bickford, Box 510, Exeter, NH 03833. Wildflowers.

Francis M. Sinclair, RFD 1, Route 85, Exeter, NH 03833. Wildflowers, ferns, and native perennials.

Mincemoyer Nursery, County Line Road, Route 526, Jackson, NJ 08527. Wildflowers, ferns, perennials, and herbs.

Woodstream Nursery, Box 510, Jackson, NJ 08527. Wildflowers and ferns.

Van Bourgondien Brothers, Box A, 245 Farmingdale Road, Route 109, Babylon, NY 11702. Wildflowers.

Martin Viette Nurseries, Route 25A, East Norwich, NY 11732. Nursery-grown wild species of perennials, ferns, shrubs, trees, and evergreens.

John Scheepers, Inc., Flower Bulb Specialists, 63 Wall St., New York, NY 10005. Native perennials, ferns, orchids, and other flowering bulbs.

Griffey's Nursery, Route 3, Box 17A, Marshall, NC 28753. Wildflowers, ferns, shrubs, vines, and bulbs.

The Three Laurels, Route 3, Box 15, Marshall, NC 28753. Wildflowers and ferns.

Gardens of the Blue Ridge, E.P. Robbins, Box 10, Pineola, NC 28662. Wildflowers, plants, shrubs, and bulbs. In business since 1892.

Sunnybrook Farms Nursery, Box 6, 9448 Mayfield Road, Chesterland, OH 44026. Wildflowers and ferns. Catalogue $1 (deductible from first order).

Bluestone Perennials, 3500 Jackson St., Mentor, OH 44060. Perennials.

Mellinger's, Inc., 2310 West South Range Road, North Lima, OH 44452. General catalogue includes wildflowers, ferns, and native trees and shrubs.

Nichols Garden Nursery, 1190 North Pacific Highway, Albany, OR 97321. Wildflowers and other plants from Oregon.

Siskiyou Rare Plants Nursery, 522 Franquette St., Medford, OR 97501. Wildflowers and ferns from the mid-coastal regions of Oregon and California.

Miles W. Fry & Sons Nursery, Route 3, Ephrata, PA 17522. Conservation plantings.

Vick's Wildgardens, Inc., Box 115, Conshohocken State Road, Gladwyne, PA 19035. Wildflowers and ferns.

Charles H. Mueller, Bulb Specialist, River Road, New Hope, PA 18938. Wildflowers and bulbs.

Beersheba's Wildflower Gardens, Beersheba Springs, TN 37305. Wildflowers and ferns.

Savage Wildflower Gardens, Box 163, McMinnville, TN 37110. Wildflowers and ferns.

Putney Nursery, Inc., Putney, VT 05346. Wildflowers, ferns, and perennials.

The Wild Garden, Box 487, Bothell, WA 98011. Wild plants.

Alpines West, Route 2, Box 259, Spokane, WA 99207. Ferns, western wildflowers, rock garden plants, and dwarf conifers and shrubs.

Woodland Acres Nursery, Route 2, Crivitz, WI 54114. Wildflowers and ferns.

L.L. Olds Seed Co., Box 7790, Madison, WI 53707. Wildflowers and ferns.

Wild Life Nurseries, Box 2724, Oshkosh, WI 54901. Plants to provide food for upland and aquatic wildlife.

BIRDS AND OTHER WILDLIFE 9

> *A simple beetle finding its way through the tall grasses, the bee that hums from flower to flower, the wood thrush singing requiem at sunset, a colony of smiling flowers with their poetic charm, a sturdy tree in the winter landscape silhouetted against the sky and telling the story of many ages, a brook with a bit of rock protruding over its edge upon which a plant climbs in a daring way to receive a little sunlight that simmers through leafy boughs—each is a world by itself, full of mystery, charm, and beauty. Each is a book of great knowledge.*
>
> Jens Jensen, *Siftings*, 1939

A squirrel scrambles to scrape up the acorns scattered around the base of an oak tree. A hummingbird flits to and fro among the plants and hovers near the honeysuckle, removing the flowers' sweet nectar. Pheasants hob-nob with two fawns. A little cottontailed rabbit scampers into the hedges and nibbles on new growth and buds. A green snake slithers silently through the grass. The pleasures of wildlife in the natural landscape are many and varied.

In at least one important respect, these animals are just like people. To attract them you have to present them with an inviting environment. For some animals this requires little or no effort. The raccoon, for example, will be attracted by the garbage you put in the can and will show its ingenuity by opening the can and spreading the garbage around your yard while it satisfies its hunger and curiosity. Other animals require more than garbage to attract them and will find your natural landscape inviting only when it presents them with food, shelter, and some sort of escape from other animals that prey on them.

Within the limits of the land's carrying capacity for each animal, animals will come to us—but only to the extent of our concern for

Fig. 9-1 *This little rabbit finds shelter for a nest in among the bushes. (Photo by Dean M. Gottehrer)*

their habits and our ability to structure our landscapes to take those habits into account. To attract chickadees to a window feeder, for example, it is important to know that they build their nests in the stumps of dead birch trees and are attracted to pine woods in the winter. Once you know that, you will build your bird feeder from a birch log and attach pine sprigs to it and around the window. When you also know that chickadees avoid strong winter winds, you will attach the pine sprigs to the windward side of the feeder to give the birds even more shelter.

There are limits to how many of any one kind of animal will be attracted to your landscape. Some animals only require a small amount of land in which to live, others need quite a bit more. You may find robins, starlings, and sparrows coming to your landscape in droves. But only one pair of whip-poor-wills will be found for every 50 acres.

Attracting birds.   Birds are the easiest animals to attract to a natural landscape of any size since they are not stopped by fences and don't require as much space in which to live as a deer does, for example.

Birds need to find food, water, and shelter for nesting, resting, and safety. If any one of these is missing in your natural landscape, the birds will be scarce. Birds get their food from a variety of sources. Seeds, nuts, fruits, berries, and flower nectar are all appetizing to different species of birds.

You should know the food value of the plants you have in your natural landscape as well as any you plan to add. Sunflowers, corn, millet, or grain sorghum will attract seed-eating birds such as goldfinches, cardinals, juncos, and sparrows. Insects will also attract birds since many birds feed on insects as well. By eating the insects, the birds help protect your landscape naturally. A chickadee will eat 200 to 500 insects a day. A brown thrasher will feast on more than 600 insects in a day, and the house wren will feed her young 500 insects a day. The reason many people are providing purple martins with nesting houses is that the purple martin eats mosquitoes and reduces that pest's population.

It is best to provide food for birds through the plantings in your landscape. That way the birds do not lose the ability to forage for themselves and do not become dependent on bird feeders. You can use feeders in the winter when food is scarce to supplement what your landscape provides naturally. You must realize, however, that feeding animals is a responsibility not to be taken lightly. Once you start to feed in the winter, the birds will become dependent on your feeder as a source of food for the entire winter when food is scarce. It is possible that birds you begin to feed will not travel south as they might otherwise do if you didn't feed them. So if you were to stop feeding in the middle of the winter, when there is no other food easily available, you could be sentencing those animals to death. If you want to use feeders, feed only when food is scarce and only as long as the scarcity lasts. And be sure to keep feeding as long as the food is scarce.

Feeding might appear to be the compassionate thing to do. Doesn't it seem more caring to feed starving deer, for example, than to allow them to starve to death? If you think about it a moment, you may see the other consequences of your actions. Keeping starving deer alive will increase the size of the herd. This diminishes the amount of food for each deer because there are now more deer. Next year even more deer will starve. Is it more compassionate to feed a starving deer or to allow the herd's size to diminish naturally and not overcrowd their feeding land?

Fig. 9-2 *Warbler*

Birds and other animals need water for drinking and bathing. If you have a stream, pool, pond, or creek on your property or nearby, you have provided them with this necessity. If you have no way of damming a stream to create a pond or digging one, perhaps a bird bath would be possible. A small pool would serve the purpose better, especially if it could be designed to blend in with the natural surroundings. But if you have no way of adding water to the natural part of your landscape, consider placing the bird bath in a more structured formal part, such as on the lawn near the house.

Hedges and shrubs, especially dense ones, provide good nesting sites for some birds. They can also provide shelter in a moment when the bird is being threatened by a natural predator. Cardinals, mockingbirds, yellow warblers, chipping and song sparrows, and catbirds are attracted to the shelter provided by hedges and shrubs.

Other birds such as robins, phoebes, chimney swifts, starlings, sparrows, house and California wrens, and sometimes barn owls are more attracted by a building in which to place their nest.

Juncos, robins, sparrows, starlings, grackles, and mourning doves love to forage for their food in a lawn. Flycatchers, nuthatches, tufted titmice, warblers, woodpeckers, finches, and grosbeaks are more attracted to a life in the woods. Ponds and streams, on the other hand, are the favored habitats of ducks, geese, herons, and wrens. Honeysuckle, dogwood, or autumn-olive hedges are ideal for cardinals, mockingbirds, and brown thrashers.

Fig. 9-3 *Eastern Bluebird*

In planning your landscape with wildlife in mind, remember that landscapes with only deciduous plantings offer no shelter for animals in the winter. That is the time they need shelter against wind and snow. They also need protection against sun and rain in the other seasons.

If you have a variety of flowers, different species of trees, and shrubs that grow to differing heights, a source of water, and open space on your landscape, you will have many more birds of many more species visiting you than if any of these were missing.

WILDLIFE AND LANDSCAPE DESIGN

When you alter the landscape, you also alter its impact on the wildlife living there or on wildlife you hope to attract. Shade trees over the side of a brook, for example, keep the brook cool enough for the trout

Fig. 9-4 *Blue Jay*

in it to survive. Remove the shade trees and the water temperature goes up. The trout seek cooler waters.

Birds are attracted to crescent-shaped clearings facing south. During the winter this is a warm place for them to bask in the sun. They drop their seeds there and the plants that grow are protective and food-bearing for the birds.

Birds also find food in seldom-mowed areas where there is a variety of grasses. The different grasses provide the birds with a variety of food. Be careful when you mow such an area. Check to see if there are nests in the grass. Mallard ducks, bobolinks, ring-necked pheasants, meadowlarks, and bobwhites, among other ground-nesting birds, like the grassy areas.

When you design your natural landscape, attempt to create as many edges between different types of environments as your land can reasonably support. This means few straight lines between trees and bushes, bushes and grasses, and so forth. The reason for this is that, as ecologists have discovered, many more animals inhabit the edge between two environments than the center of either environment.

Fig. 9-5 *Cardinal*

Dead trees may make fine firewood, and you may have to remove them in some cases where they are diseased and are endangering other trees or are endangering people walking nearby. But if you can possibly leave them standing, do so. They provide homes for many animals such as woodpeckers, chickadees, and nuthatches. Hollow trees provide shelter for raccoons, opossums, some owls, and fox squirrels.

OBSERVE NATURE IN ACTION

Naturalist Roger Tory Peterson recommends keeping a nature log and noting everything you observe about the wildlife in your yard. He suggests you include information on the animals you have seen in your property, where you saw them, and what they were doing. What plants were involved? What time of day was it? What was the weather like? Were the seasons changing? How did other animals react? Was the animal behavior new or consistent with that seen in your part of the country?

It is especially valuable to watch animal behavior when the animals are in stressful situations—threatened by natural predators or bad weather. Watching what an animal does under these circumstances may give you a clue as to what you can do to help the animal survive, without making it overly dependent on your efforts.

If you are having problems identifying animals, Peterson recommends noting down the following eight characteristics, which he says will help you identify the animal with the help of a reference book: size, shape, dominant color, special fieldmarks, behavior, movement, sound, and where the animal lives.

A nature log will force you to be more observant about the animals in your landscape and will help you see more of what the animals are doing among your plantings. Knowledge of the interaction between the animals and the landscape will help you decide how to improve what you have to offer other animals.

Don't hope to create a zoo in your backyard. Your goal should be to create an environment and landscape that animals find inviting and helpful. Whatever nature sends your way should be appreciated.

PLANTS HELPFUL TO WILD ANIMALS

Some of the plants most helpful to wildlife already exist in many landscapes. A study by the U.S. Department of the Interior's Fish and Wildlife Service indicates, for example, that the two most valuable woody plants for wildlife are oak and pine trees. There are other plants, however, that are also valuable because they provide food, shelter, or both for wild animals.

The following is a list of some of the plants that will improve your natural landscape's attraction for wild animals.

Weeds and Herbs

Amaranthus (Pigweed).   Loves the rich soil around barns and pigpens. It produces a prodigious amount of seeds; in one instance nearly 130,000 seeds were counted from one plant. An important source of food for many songbirds such as the snow bunting, Lawrence's goldfinch, junco, lark, and several varieties of sparrows. All this despite the low opinion in which many people hold this weed.

Ambrosia species (Ragweed).   Among the first weeds to creep into a field where ground has been broken. Most people haven't a good word for them—except for those who know their value to wildlife. Game birds such as the bobwhite quail and Hungarian partridge as well as songbirds such as the red-winged blackbird, easter goldfinch, junco, and a large number of different sparrows benefit from the enormous number of seeds rich in oil that ragweed provides over the winter.

Carex (Sedge).   Grows in all parts of the country, mostly in the moist soils found in bogs, marshes, and meadows. Seeds are favored by rails, grouse, swamp, tree, and Lincoln sparrows, snow buntings, and larkspurs. It is also a valuable cover plant used by nesting ducks.

Chenopodium (Goosefoot).   A group of common weeds covered with a white floury coating that provides seeds, especially late in the year, for many different kinds of songbirds such as the snow bunting, junco, common redpoll, and sparrow.

Erodium (Filaree).   Found abundantly in California and other states west of the Rockies, but rather sparsely in the East. In addition to being valuable forage for livestock, western varieties of quail, finches, and sparrows eat the seeds. Gophers, ground squirrels, and certain rodents are attracted to the seeds and foliage.

Helianthus (Sunflower).   Has a large showy flower so filled with seeds that are nutritious and appetizing to songbirds that the chances are great the birds will get to the seeds before they can be harvested for human consumption. Many songbirds, game birds, and a few rodents are attracted by sunflowers.

Panicum (Panic grass).   Widely distributed across the United States. It forms an important source of food for some ducks and geese, as well as game birds such as the ground dove and the bobwhite quail, and songbirds such as the red-winged blackbird, cowbird, smith larkspur, and several kinds of sparrows.

Polygonum (Knotweed).   Found in practically every part of the United States, although in different habitats. Some grow in hard-packed earth found in yards and alongside roads. Others grow alongside fences and field borders. Finches, larks, longspurs, and sparrows eat their seeds, as do chipmunks and ground squirrels.

Setaria species (Bristle grass).   One of the most important weeds in the country because it is so widely distributed. It occurs in fields of grain, corn, and clover as well as other open fields where the ground has been broken. Game birds such as the mourning dove, Hungarian pheasant, and bobwhite favor the seeds, as do songbirds such as the red-winged blackbird, bobolink, painted bunting, cardinal, cowbird, bickcissel, horned lark, and many different varieties of sparrows. Also favored by ground squirrels.

Stellaria media (Chickweed).   A low plant used for food by a very long list of birds. It flowers in the late winter and produces seed in early spring. Chickweed produces a large number of minute seeds.

Trees and Bushes

Acer species (Maple).   Trees that provide seeds for many birds such as the finches and grosbeaks; twigs, seeds, and bark for mammals such as squirrels, chipmunks, and beavers; and twigs and leaves for deer, elk, and moose.

Celtis (Hackberry).   A shrub or tree which may grow to 50 feet. Orange-to-purple fruit appears in September–October. Popular with cedar waxwing, yellow-bellied sapsucker, robin, and mockingbird.

Cornus (Dogwood).   Seventeen different species in the United States appear in variable forms from small to large shrubs and small trees. Leaves are strongly veined, with a red-to-bronze color in the fall; flowers are white-to-yellow and appear April–June. Fruits bunched or clustered are red, blue, or white, appearing in August–February; appreciated by wood ducks, grouse, cardinals, evening grosbeaks, robins, thrushes, vireos, cedar waxwings, and cottontail rabbits.

Crataegus species (Hawthorn).   A small-domed tree with pale-green toothed leaves. Abundant clustered white flowers bloom in May–June; a very persistent orange-to-red fruit comes in October–March. It is a favored nesting site for many birds because of the thorny dense branches that provide cover. Fruits are used mainly by fox sparrows and cedar waxwings.

Elaeagnus angustifolia (Russian olive).   A large shrub to small tree. It is an introduced species established in dry alkaline soils in the West. Small yellowish-white flowers appear in June–July and silvery-yellow-to-pink fruits are around September–February. The fruit is favored by evening grosbeaks, cedar waxwings, and robins.

Elaeagnus umbellata (Autumn olive).   A large spreading shrub with gray-green leaves; fragrant small yellowish-white flowers bloom May–July; abundant red fruits appear September–December. It provides food for many songbirds, especially the cedar waxwing, robin, and evening grosbeak.

Ilex species (Holly).   Comes in variable forms from upright rounded shrubs to small- and medium-sized trees. It has dark green leaves, evergreen or deciduous. Both male and female are needed to insure fruit, which is bright red, black, or yellow and very persistent; fruits in September–May. Many songbirds such as the thrush, mockingbird, robin, bluebird, catbird, and thrasher enjoy the fruit.

Juniperus (Cedar; juniper).   A medium-sized evergreen with dense blue-green-to-green leaves with small dusty-blue berrylike cones are in fruit September–May. Living up to its name, the cedar waxwing enjoys the fruit, as do other birds such as purple finches and grosbeaks. Robins, song sparrows, chipping sparrows, and mockingbirds use cedars for nesting, while juncos, myrtle warblers, sparrows, and other birds use the tree for roosting cover.

Lonicera tatarica (Tartarian honeysuckle).   A large shrub growing between 5 and 15 feet, with pink-to-yellow-white blooms that blossom May–June and yellow-to-red fruits that appear July–September. It is used by 18 species of birds.

Malus species (Crabapple). Small-to-medium-sized trees with showy white-to-pink blossoms that appear April–May; red, orange, or yellow fruits that are around from September to as late as April. The fruits are eaten by pheasants, cedar waxwings, purple finches, rabbits, and red fox.

Pinus species (Pine).   Ranks near the top of the list of trees important to wildlife. Pine seeds constitute more than two-thirds of the diet of three birds—the red crossbill, the Clarke nutcracker, and the white-headed woodpecker. The trees produce food for a long list of birds and mammals, shelter and nesting sites for many game and songbirds, and are favored roosting sites for migrating robins.

Prunus species (Wild cherry).   Ranges in size from shrubs to large trees. Wild black cherry occasionally reaches 100 feet. Choke cherry, pin cherry, and bitter cherry also appeal to wildlife. Small fine-toothed leaves turn yellow in fall; showy white flowers in bloom April–June. Small bright red-to-black fruits vary in their appearance with the species, generally June–November. Songbirds that eat the fruit include catbird, crow, flicker, grosbeak, kingbird, robin, starling,

Fig. 9-6 *The crabapple tree provides food for some birds, rabbits, and foxes. (Photo by Dean M. Gottehrer)*

thrasher, thrush, and cedar waxwing. The fruit also attracts raccoons, rabbits, fox, and chipmunks.

Pyracantha (Firethorn). A medium-to-large shrub with white blooms that appear in June and showy, orange-to-red fruits that appear September–March. Catbirds, mockingbirds, and purple finches will eat the firethorn fruit.

Quercus species (Oak). Grows as tall as 125 feet and produces the acorns known for being so small yet growing trees so tall. The tree also stands tall in its importance to wildlife—perhaps the most important of all. Acorns are a nutritious and abundant food used by more game and songbirds and furry, game, and small mammals than any other.

Rhus species (Sumac). Low-to-tall interestingly shaped shrubs with greenish flower spikes in bloom June–July; red-hairy conical fruit clusters are around September–May; provides an important source of food when other more desirable sources have disappeared. It is favored by a wide variety of game and songbirds, as well as rabbits and deer.

Rubus species (Blackberries; raspberries; dewberries).   Shrubs that may reach as high as 15 feet; white clustered flowers that bloom April–August; provide rose, purple, or black fruit June–September. More than 100 species of birds use these berries for food, as well as many small animals. The plants also provide effective cover and nesting sites for some birds.

Sambucus species (Elderberry).   Tall shrubs with flat white flower clusters in bloom May–July; followed by red-to-purple fruits.

Sorbus (Mountain-ash).   A medium-to-large tree; flat white flower clusters appear May–June; bright red-to-orange berry clusters in fruit August–March. The fruits are favored by some grouse, grosbeaks, and cedar waxwings.

Toxicodendron (Poison ivy; poison oak).   Plants nobody cares to have around, but they provide winter fruits for catbirds, chickadees, flickers, sapsuckers, thrushes, and woodpeckers. In spite of their irritating ways, they do provide some benefit for wildlife.

Vaccinium species (Blueberries).   Large shrubs with greenish or pink-white bell-shaped flowers in bloom May–June; provide tasty blue-black berry June–September. The berries are among the most important summer and early fall foods for grouse, scarlet tanagers, bluebirds, and catbirds; also favored by chipmunks, mice, and some deer.

Viburnum trilobum (American cranberry bush).   A tall upright shrub; showy white, flat clusters of flowers in bloom May–June; glossy scarlet clusters of fruit appear September–May. Fruits are eaten by game and songbirds.

ROCKS, 10
ROCK GARDENS,
AND
ALPINE PLANTS

There is a remarkable nobility in rocks, weatherbeaten and worn by water of past ages. Rocks, like trees, have a character all their own, and this character is emphasized when the rock is rightly placed. Usually only a few plants can be used in connection with these heralds of the past, a little moss and a few clinging plants. One should always keep in mind that the rock has a story to tell, and it should not be vulgarized by a conglomeration of unfitting plants.

Jens Jensen, *Siftings*, 1939

Rocks, stones, and pebbles add another dimension to a landscape that is difficult to include in any other way. The huge solid mass of an outcrop of local rock, the varied and different textures of naturally eroded stones, and the smooth surfaces of pebbles invite us to touch and handle them, climb on them, and loft the smaller stones and pebbles gently into a nearby stream or skip them across a pond. This attraction also works in the natural landscape.

ROCKS: RETAIN, REMOVE, OR RELOCATE?

If your grounds contain sizable rock formations, ledges, or outcrops, or if the receding glaciers have deposited boulders and smaller stones, consider yourself blessed with an added resource. Before you decide how best to employ that resource, give it some thought. Study the placement of the rocks and boulders on your grounds. Imagine how they would look if you removed all of the grass and weeds growing on and around them. How would your landscape look if you removed the rocks completely? Would your landscape present a better appearance if you moved some of the rocks to other places on your grounds?

123

Fig. 10-1 *Alpine plants in a rock garden (Photo by Dean M. Gottehrer)*

Take your time to make these judgments. You will probably decide, especially if you have outcrops or boulder-sized rocks, to leave them where they are.

Outcrops and boulders are generally so large that it is difficult, if not impossible, to remove them without great expense and effort. Although they may not be placed exactly in the location you would have chosen, they can often still be used where they are to create a center of attention in the natural landscape. It will be a place to rest and relax and to drink in the calm created by the massive and silent solidity of the rocks.

If the rocks are small enough, you may decide to move some of them to places where you feel they will be more appreciated. Removing sizable numbers of rocks is a drastic change and should rarely be considered.

One of the major assets of rocks is that they will do well in places where nothing grows. If you have a patch of land where there is little sun, poor soil, and too much or too little water for any plants to grow, you may want to move some of your rocks there. You should consider

Fig. 10-2 *Plants for the rock garden (Photo by Dean M. Gottehrer)*

Fig. 10-3 *An Alpine rock garden at the Montreal Botanical Garden (Photo by Dean M. Gottehrer)*

first the energy you will need to do this and the cost of employing someone with a machine if needed. Balance these costs against the benefits of having the rocks where you want them.

Should you add rocks to your natural landscape? Earlier in this century rock gardens were all the rage. People brought in rocks, placed them so they would appear natural, and planted alpine gardens. Now, most people don't want to go to the expense of trucking in heavy rocks. If rocks are not part of the landscape in the area around your home, they will look very much out of place if you have them brought in, but if rocks are a prominent feature of the region in which you live, and somehow your grounds did not receive their share, added stones will not look out of place. Even so, it will require time, money, and effort to place the rocks so they appear natural. You can add visual excitement to your natural landscape with materials such as plants that cost less, involve less planning and work, and produce results that are equally if not more satisfying.

Most natural landscapers choose to work with the rocks where they are. Once you have decided to work with the stone in its place,

Fig. 10-4 *The flower of the ranunculus, popularly known as the buttercup (Photo by Dean M. Gottehrer)*

you need to plan the appearance of the area. If there is any soil around or on the rocks there will probably also be plants that you don't want because they detract from the rock's natural beauty.

WORKING WITH ROCKS IN THE NATURAL LANDSCAPE

Left alone, the rocks will support the vegetation they have on and around them. If those plants are weeds to you, you will want to remove them. If those plants are wildflowers, you will probably want to leave them where they are since they have proved they can survive in a rocky environment. If the rocks support no vegetation, you may decide to change that and introduce plants that will add to the beauty the rocks contribute to your landscape.

Alpine plants.   The plants to add are those that naturally thrive and do best in a rocky environment. Alpine plants flourish in thin soil mixed with rock chips and moss. In nature, these plants grow above the timber line where the strong winds blow and the growing season is a short two to four months long. In these craggy crevices only low-

Fig. 10-5 *Sempervivum (Photo by Dean M. Gottehrer)*

growing plants will survive the wind. Alpines such as sempervivum, campanulas, and the saxifragas, to name some of the most popular ones, grow naturally on mountains below the level where there is always snow.

Alpine plants have amazingly strong root systems, which may go down five to ten feet in search of moisture and are capable of working their way into the rocks and bringing out the moisture stored there. The plants have small leaves on short stems in order to resist the wind. When the leaves die down in the winter and fall into the crevices, they create a mulch that eventually turns to compost to keep the plant healthy and protect it from outside invaders.

Annuals and other fleshy soft plants cannot survive the alpine plant's environment. The cold alien nature of the mountains requires plants that are hardy and live a long life. It takes a great effort for a plant to become established in rocky mountainous places. Annuals don't live long enough to do it. Alpines, on the other hand, thrive on adversity and hardship makes them grow strong. They love the wind, cold, and starvation. The soft self-indulgent life, with too much food, too long a growing season, and too easy an access to water, turns them into weaklings unable to long survive.

To make sure your rock plants thrive with a minimum amount of care, you need to provide them with the proper conditions for growth. Many of these plants, if given a good deal of attention, will still prosper if even in less than ideal growing places. But our object is to avoid as much maintenance as possible. Although all these plants require some attention since they are out of their natural environment (unless you live above the timber line and below the snow line), the

Fig. 10-6 *Sedum (Photo by Dean M. Gottehrer)*

amount of attention they need can be reduced if you choose the right places for them.

The best location for alpine and rock plants is on a sloping hill with a northeastern exposure. This location provides enough sun, but not too much. If exposed to the full summer sun, and soaked with high humidity, alpine plants will literally be cooked and will degenerate into a mildewed mass. The northeastern sloping hill reduces the amount of summer sunlight and also the variations in thaw and freeze. Constant freezing and thawing is something they are not subjected to in their natural mountain environs and it will damage the plants. Any plants heaved by a thaw should be replaced in the ground as soon as the earth is workable.

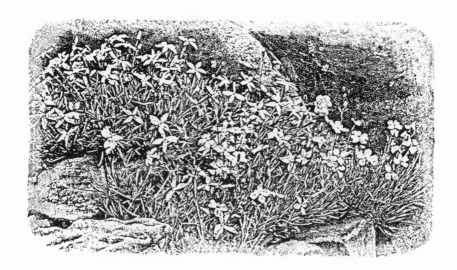

Fig. 10-7 *Cheddar Pink*

The worst soil for alpine plants is clay. It packs too hard around the roots, which need plenty of air around them. A very sandy or gravelly soil is also bad because it drains too quickly. The best soil for alpine and rock plants is a coarse gritty soil, capable of holding water for a long time for the roots to take it in, yet a short enough time so that the roots are not moisture laden. When you are using alpines around the base of any rocks, a layer of hard clay a foot to a foot and a half below the surface will serve as an underground water basin to supply the plants with moisture.

While alpines like a proper supply of moisture, they don't like a humid, moist growing place. Alpines, especially those with downy gray leaves, cannot tolerate having their foliage resting on a humid moist soil. They do better on rocks. If your rocks are under trees, you should use other types of plants than alpines. The climate under a tree is usually too moist. In the winter the soggy leaves will cause the plants to rot if the leaves are not raked up. Avoid trees with extensive and shallow root systems such as maples, willows, ashes, elms, poplars, and linden. These trees will compete with the alpines for moisture and nutrients and the trees will win. Alpines generally cannot take very much strong competition. They are used to difficulties

Fig. 10-8 *Dianthus*

from the climate, but not from other vegetation. Instead of using deciduous trees to provide summer shade, as might seem logical, use small coniferous shrubs nearby if you need to increase protection from the full summer sun. Any deciduous trees that cast shade over the areas where you have alpine plants should be far enough away so that their leaves don't drop onto the rock plants.

Although alpines like a well-drained soil, they also need to be watered frequently the first summer until their roots have penetrated deeply into the rock or soil. Don't turn a hose on the plants—that's the equivalent of hitting them with a hurricane. Use a fine spray nozzle or a sprinkling can to produce a fine mist that gently settles on the plants. Hard torrents of water will damage the plants and erode valuable soil from on top of the rocks. After the first or second summer, when the plants are firmly established, it should not be necessary to water the plants unless there is a drought in your area.

Fertilizing these plants is generally not necessary. If you do decide to feed your alpines, don't use fresh manure or any other strong fertilizer. It will kill the plants. The best dressing is a well-rotted animal manure, which will slowly feed the plants.

Fig. 10-9 *Androsace*

Well-established alpine and rock plants don't need weeding. They are close enough together to prevent weeds from getting a hold on the soil. Their leaves will also provide a mulch that prevents weeds from appearing. But until the alpines become well-established it would be wise to pull any weeds as they show up. If the weeds are allowed to establish roots, you may have to remove the rock to get rid of them. Weeding is necessary the first and maybe the second year after alpines are planted.

If you live in a climate of hard winters, especially where there is an early snow that stays on the ground until late in the spring, you don't have to worry about the alpines making it through the winter. They do best when constantly covered with snow. If you live in a climate where snow comes and goes during the winter, you probably should protect your alpines—not from the cold but from the warmth. A cover of evergreen boughs, hay, or any other light and airy material should be applied after the ground freezes hard and kept on until the ground defrosts and there is little or no chance of a late freeze. This covering will keep the plants cold through the winter and protect them from heaving and the other dangers of a thaw–freeze–thaw cycle.

Rock gardens. The old theory about rock gardens was that they should be placed out of sight from the house, behind a hedge, or on

Fig. 10-10 *Gentiana*

the other side of a hill. The rock garden was one of those accidental delights a person was supposed to happen upon, perhaps at the end of a horse ride or a walk in the woods. They were not really accidents—it was all a charade. There is no reason to place alpine and rock plants out of sight from the house, unless the rocks are out of sight from the house already. You should be conscious, however, that as small plants with small flowers they fare poorly in comparison with larger plants and flowers. They should be placed somewhere out of competition with perennials, bulbs, or other large plants that will directly detract from their delicate beauty. It is also important to place them so the observer can get close to them. Their small size makes a smaller scale and a shorter viewing distance helpful in showing off their beauty.

It was also traditional in alpine and rock gardens to plant the taller plants in low areas and reduce the plant height as the altitude increased. This principle was derived from observing nature. The tallest alpine plants are at the lower altitudes. On level or nearly level ground, this means that the tall plants will obscure the shorter plants

Fig. 10-11 *Leontopodium Alpinum*

and will prevent you from viewing the blooms in back. There is no reason to do this. You should plant the taller plants in the back and the shorter ones in front for a pleasing visual display.

If you look at books on alpine gardens you will see colorful displays of a myriad of plants in a small area. Resist the temptation to plant so many plants that they grow together into a carpet of alpines. In nature you don't find these carpets of color and beauty. To get such growth you have to plant the plants some distance apart and allow them to spread out over the years. Remember what Jensen said at the beginning of this chapter. The fewer alpines you have, the more attention they will receive and the more appreciated they will be. Also, the fewer you have, the more natural they will appear. The plants are more isolated because they have a more difficult environment in which to survive.

ALPINE AND ROCK PLANT SELECTION

A complete and exhaustive listing of the various genera and species of different alpine and rock plants would fill a book. (Several books with such detailed listings are found in the bibliography.) The following lists provide some ideas of the types of plants best used by beginners (because they are fairly hardy and easy to grow) and other plants suited to special planting situations.

Plants for Beginners

Plant	Color of Bloom	Blooming Season
Achillea	White-to-yellow	May to mid-September
Aethionema	White-to-pale-pink	May and June
Allium	Blue through yellow and pink-to-white	Spring and summer
Alyssum	White-to-pale yellow	April to July
Androsace	Red and white	May to July
Anemone	Red, pink, white, purple	April through June
Antennaria dioica rosea	White or pink	May and June
Anthemis	Yellow or white	May to August
Arabis	White, pink, purple,	April to June
Armeria	White-to-pink	May to June
Aster	All colors but yellow	May to November
Campanula	White, blue, violet, pink	May to September
Cerastium	White	April to October
Corydalis	Yellow, red, lavender	May through August
Cyclamen	Pink, white, reddish	August to May
Dianthus	Pink, rose, white	May to July
Draba aizoides	Yellow	April
Dryas	Yellow or white	May
Epilobium	Rose, pink, purple	July
Erinus alpinus	Purple	May to June
Erodium	White, pink, yellow, red, or purple	April to June
Genista	Yellow	May and June
Gentiana	Blue	Late spring to November

Plant	Color of Bloom	Blooming Season
Geranium	White, pink, red, violet	May to July
Gypsophila	White-to-pink	May to October
Helianthemum	Pink, copper	Early and late summer
Iberis	White, red, purple	April to frost
Leontopodium alpinum	Yellow	July and August
Nepeta mussini	Lavender-blue	Early and late summer
Pentstemon	Blue, violet, purple, red	June to August
Phlox	White-to-pink and lavender	April to September
Potentilla	White, yellow, red	May to August
Primula	Almost every color	April and May
Pulmonaria	Blue, red, white, violet	Early spring
Ranunculus	Yellow, red, pink, orange, white	April to August
Saxifraga	Pink, red, yellow, white, purple	March to May
Sedum	White, yellow, pink, red, purple	May to October
Sempervivum	Green, yellow, red	June
Silene	Red, white, pink	June to October
Sisyrinchium	Blue or yellow	April to July
Thymus	White, red, lilac, purple pink	Late May
Tunica	Pink-to-pale purple	Summer and fall
Veronica	Blue, purple	April to October

Plants for Hot, Dry, Full Sun Locations

Plant	Color of Bloom	Blooming Season
Acaena	Inconspicuous	—
Achillea	White-to-yellow	May to mid-September
Actinea	Yellow	Early summer
Aethionema	White-to-pale pink	May and June
Alyssum	White-to-pale yellow	April to July

Plant	Color of Bloom	Blooming Season
Anacyclus	White	Early summer
Androsace	Red and white	May to July
Antennaria	White or pink	May and June
Anthemis	Yellow or white	May to August
Arabis	White, pink, purple	April to June
Armeria	White-to-pink	May to June
Arnebia	Yellow, maroon	May
Artemisia	White, yellow	July to September
Aubrieta	Red-to-purple	April to June
Callirhoë	Pink-to-purple	June to August
Campanula	White, blue, violet, pink	May to September
Cerastium	White	April to October
Cheiranthus	Yellow, gold, red, brown	Late spring
Coreopsis	Yellow, pink, purple	June to August
Cytisus	Yellow, white, purple	May to June
Dianthus	Pink, rose, white	May to July
Douglasia	Red, yellow, purple, lilac	April and May
Draba	White, orange, yellow	April to May
Dryas	Yellow or white	May
Edraianthus	Blue, violet	May to July
Erigeron	White-to-purple with yellow centers	June to October
Erinus	Purple	May to June
Eriogonum	Yellow	May to July
Eriophyllum	Yellow	Summer
Erodium	White, pink, yellow, red, purple	April to June
Erysimum	Orange, yellow, lilac	Spring
Euphorbia	White, yellow	April to October
Genista	Yellow	May and June
Gypsophila	White-to-pink	May to October
Hebe	White-to-pink, lilac	July to September
Helianthemum	Pink, copper	Early and late summer
Helichrysum	White, orange, red, yellow	Mid-September to frost

Plant	Color of Bloom	Blooming Season
Hieracium	Yellow, orange-to-red	May to September
Hypericum	Yellow	July to August
Iberis	White, red, purple	April to frost
Inula	Yellow	July to September
Lavandula	Blue-to-violet	August and September
Lewisia	White or red	Early spring
Linum	Blue or yellow	June to August
Malvastrum	Red	Summer
Micromeria	White, pink-to-purple	July to fall
Oenothera	Yellow, white, pink	June to August
Opuntia	Yellow, scarlet	June and July
Papaver	Red, yellow, pink, scarlet	May and June
Paronychia	Inconspicuous	—
Pentstemon	Blue, violet, purple, red	June to August
Phlox	White-to-pink and lavender	April to September
Physaria	Yellow	Early summer
Potentilla	White, yellow, red	May to August
Raoulia	Yellow	Spring
Salvia	Blue, violet, red, white	August to September
Saponaria	Rose, pink	May to August
Scabiosa	Blue, purple, rose, white, yellow	June to September
Sedum	White, yellow, pink, red, purple	May to October
Sempervivum	Green, yellow, red	June
Sisyrinchium	Blue or yellow	April to July
Stachys	White or violet	July to frost
Talinum	Yellow, pink, red	Late spring and summer
Tanacetum	Yellow	Summer
Thlaspi	White, lilac	April to May
Thymus	White, red, lilac, purple, pink	Late May

Plant	Color of Bloom	Blooming Season
Townsendia	White and pink	Late spring
Tunica	Pink-to-pale purple	Summer and fall
Valeriana	White-to-pink or lavender	June to August
Veronica	Blue, purple	April to October

Plants for Partial or Full Shade

Plant	Color of Bloom	Blooming Season
Actaea	White	April to June
Ajuga	Blue, white	May and June
Anemone	Red, pink, white, purple	April to August
Anemonella	White	May and June
Arum	White	April to August
Asarum	Purple or brown	March to May
Asperula	Pink, white, blue, red	Early spring
Astilbe	White, pink, red, purple	June to August
Bergenia	Pink, white, purple	Early spring
Brunnera	Blue	Spring
Cassiope	White to red	May to June
Chimaphila	White, pink	Summer
Chrysogonum	Yellow	April to June
Claytonia	White-to-pink	Early spring
Coptis	White	April to July
Cyclamen	Pink, white, red	December to May
Cymbalaria	Blue, lavender, mauve	May to November
Dalibarda	White	Summer
Dicentra	Greenish-white, pink	May to frost
Dodecatheon	White, purple, yellow, red	April to June
Epimedium	Red, yellow, violet, white	May to July
Galax	White	May to June
Gaultheria	White-to-pink	May to June
Gaylussacia	White	May to June
Goodyera	White	July to August
Haberlea	Lilac	May

Plant	*Color of Bloom*	*Blooming Season*
Helleborus	White, green, purple	Late fall or winter
Hepatica	Bluish-white, lilac	March to June
Jeffersonia	White	Summer
Linnaea	Pink	June to July
Liriope	Lilac, purple, white	July to September
Mahonia	Yellow	April to May
Mimulus	Yellow, copper, pink	June and July
Mitchella	Pinkish-white	Summer
Mitella	White	Late spring
Moneses	White	June to August
Omphalodes	Blue, white	April and May
Orchis	Pink, violet	May to July
Pachysandra	White-to-purple	April to May
Phlox	White-to-pink and lavender	April to September
Primula	Almost every color	April and May
Pulmonaria	Blue, red, white, violet	Early spring
Pyrola	White, pink, purple	June to August
Ramonda	Purple	May to June
Sarcococca	White	Mid-spring
Saxifraga	Pink, red, yellow, white, purple	March to May
Shortia	White	May and June
Synthyris	White, pale blue-to-blue-purple	April to May
Tanakaea	Greenish-white	May
Thalictrum	Yellow, lilac-purple, white	May to August
Tiarella	White	April to July
Trillium	Greenish, white, pink	March to June
Uvularia	Yellow	Spring and early summer
Vancouveria	White	May and June

PATHS AND 11
PLAY AREAS

The attraction and pleasure gained from a walk in the woods has become a part of our language. "To be led down the garden path" is to be enticed into a pleasureful experience so grand that disillusionment is inevitable. It would be wise to remember that too often the promise of the garden path is not fulfilled.

A walkway or path serves several purposes in a natural landscape. The lawn you turned into a meadow, the spectacular view of the countryside, your oldest tree, the inviting stone bench alongside your pond, and a patch of wildflowers in bloom are all worthless unless you have a way of getting to them. The path serves to connect these points of interest. It can also determine the order in which you and your guests experience the attractions in your natural landscape.

Many people find that paths are a way to relax, to take in the pleasures of nature, and to work off some of the daily stresses. No matter how many times they walk the same path, they find fresh interest in a plant they had never noticed before, a tree they hadn't quite appreciated, a bird call they had never heard.

STRUCTURING A PATH

The straight line of high school geometry may be the shortest distance between two points, but a good path is the *best possible route* between two or more points. The shortest distance between two points on your landscape may run straight up a hill. A path there, besides causing erosion, would force you and your guests to demonstrate your mountaineering skills. Let your path follow the land's contours as it gently climbs the slope. You will discover that your path is well worth the extra distance.

The benefits of your path ought to be obvious to its users, otherwise they will soon make a new path on either side of yours. Any

141

Fig. 11-1 *A pathway through the landscape, bordered with azaleas in bloom (Photo by Dean M. Gottehrer)*

dangers along the way should be minimized so that walkers can devote their full attention to enjoying nature and the scenery and not wonder whether or not they will make it across the makeshift bridge in front of them.

Unlike today's modern superhighways, which move us from one place to another as fast as the current speed limit will allow, paths are not meant to simply move us from one place to another, but to provide enjoyment along the way. If the *Canterbury Tales* had been written as a travelogue of a pilgrimage to Canterbury, they would have been rather dull. But as a story of how the travelers entertained themselves along the way, they have survived the passage of centuries and still hold our interest and attention.

If your grounds are filled with trees, bushes, and very little open space, you must look upon your landscape as a solid mass through which you will carve out a space to travel in. If your property has more open space than woods, you must view the space as an empty platform on which you will have to place plants or other materials to delineate the path. Bushes and trees will define the pathway.

The materials you can use to construct paths and walkways include grass, stone (flagstone and stepping stone), gravel, brick, sand, pine needles, wood (logs, cross sections, rails, and chips), bark, and concrete. Your choice will depend on your purpose. You hardly would use concrete for a path through the woods. Nor would you use pine needles for a path from the garage to the kitchen door.

The best paths are those that blend in and seem to be a natural part of the landscape. In some areas, simply walking a path several times is enough to compact the vegetation and make it obvious that there is a pathway there. In other places you may have to mow, cut, chop, and kill plants to clear the way.

Before you design a pathway, observe your landscape for at least a year. Explore your property well during the different seasons. Perhaps you want more visible color from wildflowers in the spring or a better view of the valley in the fall. Perhaps you need a cleared southern exposure in the winter and cool climate under a pine tree in the summer. All these may be aspects of your landscape to consider in locating the path through your property. It is especially important to observe your property in winter when the leaves are off the trees. The views are more open and may give you ideas of what trees to clear for the view in the summer. You may want to keep the trees, but clear away some of the lower branches to create a tunnel-like effect with sunlight at the end.

When you design your pathways, remember to include a variety of attractions—different kinds of plants, views, flowers, and so forth. And let there be a variety of walking experiences. The path should have some straight sections, others that curve, and still others that zig-zag. Avoid right angles where a curve will be a shortcut. If you don't incorporate the obvious shortcuts into your path your guests probably will. If your property is extensive, lay out your paths to provide walks of varying lengths, and provide opportunities to cut a walk short.

Avoid sharply defined edges of your paths—they look unnatural. A brick walkway with a grass border to be trimmed is not nature's way. Bricks may have their place in other more formal circumstances, but in a natural landscape brick and concrete require far too much time and money and too great a maintenance effort to keep up. Your pathways should be wide enough to be inviting (three feet is the narrowest they can be without making your guests feel claustrophobic; four to five feet is better) but not so wide as to be lacking in structure.

Fig. 11-2 *Walkway in a natural landscape design by Jens Jensen (Courtesy of Leonard K. Eaton and University of Michigan, College of Architecture Library)*

If you have fairly flat grounds, you will have no problem with water, unless your land is low-lying. But if your property is hilly any path you construct will have to be designed with water-flow in mind. In a poorly designed path both people and water alike will be taking the same course and the people will soon be discouraged from walking there. A well-designed path will allow for water runoff. This is accomplished by raising the center of the path, creating a small channel alongside the path to carry off the water, and controlling the water as it flows down the hillside through these channels. If the area where you wish to place your path has spots that are damp or wet—marsh or bogland as opposed to running water—you can use another device to solve the problem. Construct a corduroy trail by placing logs across the pathway touching each other. Pack earth on top of the logs. The soil prevents the wood from rotting by keeping air and organisms away from the wood.

With enough land and a diverse number of settings, you can consider types of trails other than those for walking or hiking. Trails for cross-country skiing, bicycling, horseback riding, snowmobiles, and trailbikes have all been designed. But if you are intent on protecting the peaceful serenity of your natural landscape, you should think long and hard before you construct trails for snowmobiles and trailbikes. Try to discourage your family from owning these vehicles. If that's not possible, it is better to restrict their use to a portion of your property where you have constructed a trail specifically for them.

Once you have established a path or trail, it is important to keep it in good condition. If you allow weeds to overgrow it, or ignore the litter that mysteriously builds up, or forget to trim back tree branches and bushes that get in the way, it won't be used very much. Keeping a path well-maintained requires only a few hours a year, but that investment will be well worth the many hours of enjoyment the path will provide you, your family, and your guests.

NATURAL PLAY AREAS FOR CHILDREN AND ADULTS

In a sense, your entire natural landscape should be viewed as one huge recreation area where people come to nature with their play. Children climb trees, race down the garden paths, and play hide and seek among the bushes. Adults study and admire the wildflowers and other plants, spend lazy afternoons alongside the creek, and wander together to and fro. All of this can be considered play. A well-designed natural landscape will entice both children and adults to spend much time enjoying its attractions. What about areas specifically designed for play? How does nature fit in here?

One of the most obvious examples is the way trees are used as play areas. An old tire suspended from a sturdy limb makes a fine swing for children. Trees with strong low branches will easily support a growing youngster who desires to develop climbing skills. Tree houses have long been childhood refuges from the intrusion of adults.

Set aside part of your grounds where children can interact with nature without stepping on fragile alpine plants or wildflowers. Include the children when you plan the area. Decide what trees they would like to remain, what plants they would like to care for, and what kinds of flowers they might enjoy. Steer them toward plants that are easy to grow and care for.

In planning where to place a child's play area, keep in mind that small children tend to play close to the main entrance of the house. Therefore, it is wise to locate their special play area near that door. The parent supervising the children should be able to see them from the house. It also helps to remember that older children will play wherever they want to unless you have brought them up to recognize certain areas as off-limits. You won't want them tromping over delicate plants, so make it clear to them that they are to keep their play confined to a designated area.

Children will be attracted to spots that have the most to offer them. Recognize this and structure their play area with a variety of levels, places to play, and different play activities. Have a hard play surface nearby, since many children's games and play activities require a hard surface—tricycles, bicycles, ball games, jump rope, jacks, and hopscotch. In fact, many studies indicate that children will play more frequently on a hard surface than on the grass when given a choice.

If children are provided with an environment rich in choice, they will create their own opportunities. Anyone who has ever been to the beach with a child will recognize the truth of that. At the shore, the only play possibilities, other than the toys the child brings, are the water and the sand. Yet out of that comes an assortment of activities from swimming and wading to collecting sea shells and building sand castles. When you create a natural play area for children, place the raw materials of nature there. Include soil, dead wood, leaves, rocks, insects, plants, sand, and so forth. Children will make their own use of these to create something unique and fulfilling for themselves.

Nothing quite as all-involving can be created for adults. They will receive most of their pleasure from being present in a natural area and exploring it. If you plan to construct something for adults you will

have to depend on traditional landscaping devices—picnic areas, terraces, patios, volleyball and tennis courts, putting greens, swimming
pools, and so forth. It is best to separate these from each other to preserve the natural appearance of your landscape, since putting them all
in one area would create a focus you may not want. Picnic tables
should be placed under the tall trees for shady coolness in the summer. Patios and terraces should be located where trees, bushes, and
shrubs serve as surrounding walls. Ball courts can be hidden behind a
screen of trees and shrubs.

The council ring.   A play structure developed by landscape architect
Jens Jensen for children and adults together is the council ring. This
area blends unobtrusively with the natural landscape and can provide
hours of entertainment and enjoyment.

> *Just below "Players Hill," on the slope of the ravine, the first council
> ring was built—a new adventure. In this friendly circle, around the fire,
> man becomes himself. Here there is no social caste. All are on the same
> level, looking each other in the face. A ring speaks of strength and friend-
> ship and is one of the great symbols of mankind. The fire in the center
> portrays the beginning of civilization, and it was around the fire our
> forefathers gathered when they first placed foot on this continent. . . .
> The smoke of the fire, illuminated by the moon, forms fantastic shapes
> which gently float over the deep and penetrating shadows of the ravine.
> Many of these rings have I built since this first attempt. When they are
> placed on school grounds or in playfields, I call them story rings. These
> rings are the beginning of a new social life in the gardens of the America
> of tomorrow.*
>
> Jens Jensen, *Siftings*, 1939

Jensen's ring is a formalized version of the campfire. In the center
is placed a hearth, where people can start their own campfires. The
ring is a circle built of fieldstone, sometimes put together with mortar,
sometimes not. The circle is usually about 15 feet in diameter, but it
can be any size that fits in with your property, as long as the seating
part is not too close to the fire. The fieldstone is built up to about one
and a half to two and a half feet. It is just high enough so that people
can sit on top of it. The top layer of fieldstone is made of flat-surfaced
pieces.

The council rings were usually located in the back part of the
property in or near a corner where they would be as far removed from
the street and passing traffic as possible. Jensen usually surrounded

Fig. 11-3 *Council ring by Jens Jensen (Courtesy of Leonard K. Eaton and University of Michigan, College of Architecture Library)*

them with trees; a path usually led to a break in the circle. If there is more than one path, there should be more than one break. Too many breaks destroys the continuity and intimacy of the council ring.

The ring has all of the pleasures of the campfire and more. Whereas the campfire has only a center, the ring has an outside structure and is protected and strong because of it. The ring attracts and contains people whereas the campfire only attracts. Jensen felt his rings were very democratic structures. They were very much in place in the prairies of Illinois where he built them.

In the natural landscape Jensen's rings provide space for entertaining friends on warm summer evenings, or welcoming the spring with a friendly inviting blaze to warm the participants. And they need very little maintenance—only removal of the ashes and cleaning up any debris.

Fig. 11-4 *Council ring with steps designed by Jens Jensen (Courtesy of Leonard K. Eaton and University of Michigan, College of Architecture Library)*

OUTDOOR LIGHTING

Certain areas around the home benefit from outdoor lighting. Walkways, driveways, pools, patios, terraces, steps, parking areas and slopes are all much safer when they are lit up at night. Beyond a consideration for safety, should you consider using outdoor lights to highlight the natural landscape? The answer must be one of personal taste and budget. Installing outdoor lighting of trees and bushes, for example, is expensive, especially if the lights are placed close to the plantings away from the house.

In the past few years the price of electricity has increased steadily with no end in sight. So you must decide whether the use you will make of the lights justifies the expense. A less costly solution is to attach the lights on the house, directing them at only those parts of the

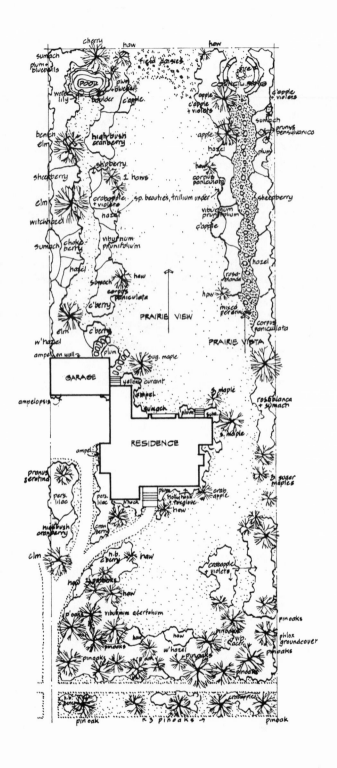

outdoors closest to the house. This saves on wiring for the installation and on the fixtures, because lights mounted on the house are less expensive than ones used for concealed outdoor lighting.

If budget is not a consideration, and you have a home that has large windows or glass doors opening on the rear, use floodlights and spotlights to draw attention to certain areas of your natural landscape from inside. This type of lighting is unusually effective in the North during a late-night snowstorm when one can watch from inside the flakes falling, accumulating, and turning the landscape white.

◀ **Fig. 11-5** *Landscape design showing council ring at upper right corner. Design by Jens Jensen. (Courtesy of Leonard K. Eaton and University of Michigan, College of Architecture Library)*

PESTS AND 12
OTHER
PROBLEMS

Out for a walk in your natural landscape one early spring afternoon you spy an aphid on the leaf of your prized plant. Looking about further you see mites on another plant. As you scout around more you see insects all about you. Your landscape is infested, you think. What should you do? If you're like most people, you run for the insecticide.

And that's the problem. The insecticide, for the most part, will kill not only all of the bugs that were driving you mad, but also the bugs that were doing the work you wanted the insecticide to do.

Entomologists have identified some 750,000 insect species. Of these 10,000 are known to be pests. Insects damage plants in one of four ways. Beetles, caterpillars, inchworms, and grasshoppers feed on the leaves. Aphids, scale insects, mites, leafhoppers and lace and mealy bugs pierce the plant and suck out the juice, causing damage to the plant tissue and perhaps death. The common stalk borer bores into the woody parts of plants. Finally insects such as cutworms feed on the roots and other parts of the plant at the soil line.

Insects become pests when they do enough damage to prevent a plant from developing normally—at their worst, they kill the plant. Ironically, pest invasions usually occur only on land that is or has been cultivated. Insects seen in virgin forests become pests on cultivated lands. The reason cultivated lands are sometimes pest-ridden is that they are often planted with only one crop which may not have been rotated, and the lands are extensively treated with pesticides to get rid of the bugs and preserve the crop.

Yet many insects are beneficial to the natural landscaper. These are the predators—of other insects. The ladybug, praying mantis, aphis lion, lacewing, and some species of wasps will help reduce the

Fig. 12-1 *Lady bug*

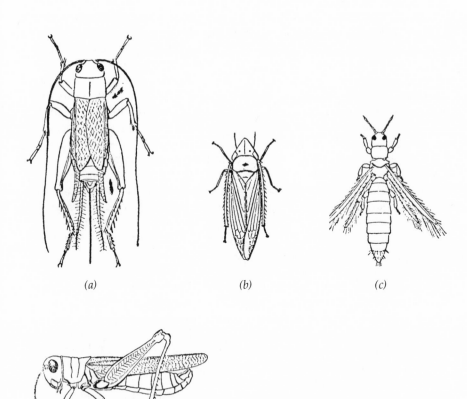

(a)   *(b)*   *(c)*

(d)

Fig. 12-2 *a) Cricket, b) Leafhopper, c) Thrips, d) Grasshopper*

number of unwanted insects. Along with the pest predators, more than 1,000 viruses, bacteria, fungi, rickettsia, and nematodes attack insects and help keep them under control.

CHEMICAL PESTICIDES: YES OR NO?

Should you use chemical pesticides to control unwanted insects? Only in an emergency or as a last resort. The use of some pesticides is a little bit like dropping an atom bomb on your neighbor's house to quiet a noisy party. Instead of reducing the irritation, you have eliminated it *and* the neighbor who gave you a helping hand when you were in trouble. Some pesticides are overkill. They remove wanted and unwanted insects without discrimination.

Other pesticides, such as DDT have proved to be dangerous to human and other animal life by hanging in the atmosphere so long that they literally poisoned the environment. And, although using only a small amount on your land may not seem harmful, everyone's small amount adds up to a lot all over the country. You don't have to worry about DDT, since it is no longer available, but what about the effects of other pesticides? It is possible that after further study they too will be found to be harmful. Why take a chance with pesticides when you have other more natural alternatives—for example, the praying mantis? The only reason would be that natural pest predators take time to establish.

If you do use chemical pesticides, it is important for your safety and the safety of others, as well as for the good of the environment, that you follow all the rules in Chapter Two for herbicide use. The rules are the same for herbicides and pesticides because the dangers are similar. In addition, the following should be observed:

Use granular formulations because they are less hazardous.

Apply pesticides in the evening when bees aren't active.

Use the lowest effective dose of the pesticide.

Apply only when necessary.

To apply a chemical pesticide successfully so that it doesn't kill too many beneficial insects, you must know several things. First, you must know the pest's life cycle, how and when it is born, how long it lives, and when the best time is to attack it with a pesticide. You should also know the pest's habits—where and when it seeks food, what it eats, and if the food can be poisoned. What are the pest's natural enemies? When do they occur? What are their habits? Will the pesticide kill them or are there times when they are less affected? What is the host plant? Will it be damaged by the pesticide? How can it be protected?

There is no single time when it is best to apply a pesticide. Sometimes it is better to use it when the pest first appears, other times when there are certain numbers, or sometimes at a particular stage of pest development. Since there are no general rules, consult your local agricultural extension service.

One of the best times to apply a pesticide is when the pest's natural predator is not going to be affected by the chemical. For example, aphids, scale insects, and mites usually appear in early spring. By applying chemicals for scale control before the plants grow, and for mite and aphid control early in the season, you increase your chances of not destroying the natural predators of these pests at the same time.

Follow the chemical's instructions for correct mixing. Use the proper dose and apply it in the right place. Some chemicals, for example, are not sprayed on the plant but are applied to the roots where they are taken in by the plant and kill the insects that feed on the leaves.

AN OUNCE OF PREVENTION

There are several ways you can prevent insect pests from becoming more numerous and killing your plants. Many insects winter over in plant parts and debris from the previous growing season. Each fall clean up those parts of your natural landscape where debris isn't being used as mulch, compost, or wild animal shelter. This will reduce the number of places where insects can pass through the winter.

Purchase disease-free pest-resistant plants and seeds. Weak plants are subject to more problems from disease and pests than strong ones. Seek strong healthy plants and put them in a fertile well-drained soil. Poor soil produces a poorly developed plant, which is then subject to attack from disease and pests. Seed treated for decay and damping-off is more resistant than seed that has not been treated. Destroy diseased plants immediately, before they have a chance to infect other plants. Burn them if possible. Prune off diseased parts of plants that can be saved (make your cut well below the infection). Disinfect the pruning tools and paint the pruning wounds. Destroy the pruned-off diseased parts. Destroy any diseased leaves and flowers of woody plants when they fall.

NATURAL ALTERNATIVES TO PEST CONTROL

The object in dealing with pesty insects is not to remove them completely from your landscape but to control them. They may drive you buggy, but as long as they don't get out of control they do serve a useful function—as food for other insects, birds, and animals.

Once you decide to use natural methods to control the pest population, you must also accept the fact that you will have some chewed-up leaves and some destroyed plants—a preferred alternative to the extensive damage you would incur by the wholesale use of pesticides, to say nothing of the damage to the environment. Also, once you decide not to use pesticides, you will not need to buy, clean, wash, or store the equipment.

The main alternatives to chemical pesticides are insect predators, birds and other animals, and botanical pesticides.

Insect predators.   The two most important insect predators are the praying mantis and the ladybug. The praying mantis will eat grasshoppers, crickets, locusts, wasps, bees, aphids, leafhoppers, tent caterpillars, chinch bugs, beetles, flies, and spiders.

The ladybug will eat aphids, mealybugs, whiteflies, spider mites, scale insects, and the eggs of other insects. The average adult ladybug can eat 400 aphids a week. The ladybugs themselves are prolific reproducers. One mating will produce between 200 and 1,000 ladybugs.

The aphis lions (ant lions, dobson flies, and lace wings) will feed on aphids, mealybugs, thrips, scale insects, whiteflies, moth eggs, and caterpillars. Damselbugs will eat aphids, scale insects, and thrip.

Ladybugs and praying mantises are easily purchased commercially. Their containers can be stored until ready for use. The native ladybugs and praying mantises you find in your own landscape have only one advantage over those you buy commercially. The native ladybugs and praying mantises are much more likely to remain on your property than those you purchase. However, the chances are fairly good that you will have enough pests for these predators to feed on, and as long as there is food for them they will stay. Be sure not to create a predator population since it will reduce the pest levels so low that the predators will have to look elsewhere for food. Commercial suppliers can provide information on the proper number of ladybugs and praying mantises needed for your area.

Birds.   Birds are even more important in pest control than insect predators. Some birds have a voracious appetite for insects and live

Fig. 12-3 *Praying mantis eating grasshopper*

on little else. Chickadees, house wrens, brown thrashers, and phoebes are the best birds to have around because their diets are composed mainly of insects. Robins, bluebirds, and woodpeckers are also good helpers. Swallows eat nocturnal insects.

The Baltimore oriole will eat caterpillars, beetles, ants, grasshoppers, wasps, and spiders. Cuckoos will feed on hairy and tent caterpillars, beetles, grasshoppers, stinkbugs, crickets, and spiders.

Insects form part of the diet of many birds that also eat seeds and fruits. In addition to the birds mentioned above, the following birds are also insect-eaters and will help keep a balance between pest and

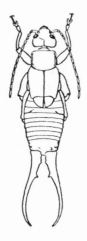

Fig. 12-4 *Earwig*

predator insects in the natural landscape: blackbirds, creepers, crows, flycatchers, mockingbirds, nuthatches, sparrows, swifts, tanagers, Texas kingfishers, thrushes, titmice, vireos, warblers, and whip-poor-wills.

More than half the food of some 1,400 North American bird species consists of insects. You can see why it is important, then, not to eradicate the insects with chemical pesticides. Most birds feed their young a diet of insects early in the spring. It is not unusual for birds to rescue an area being infested with insects. In 1925, for example, a plague of locusts ended when birds gathered and ate enough locusts to reduce their numbers. Use the techniques described in Chapter Nine to attract birds to your natural landscape. Not only will the birds provide visual delight, they will also patrol the area to eliminate unwanted insects.

Toads, frogs, salamanders, turtles, snakes, badgers, pheasants, skunks, mice, moles, squirrels, and chickens will also help remove unwanted insects. Toads are especially voracious consumers of insects. One toad will eat up to 10,000 insects in three months. The toad's diet will consist of cutworms, grubs, crickets, rose beetles, squash bugs, caterpillars, ants, army worms, chinch bugs, gypsy moth caterpillars, sow bugs, moths, flies, mosquitoes, and slugs.

Botanical pesticides. These insecticides are made from plants, not from chemicals. Be certain when you purchase them to look at the label, since some processors are adding chemicals to the plant matter. Botanical insecticides were used prior to the first use of chemical insecticides. They were developed when it was observed that certain plants and plant parts were not attacked by insects. The advantages of the botanicals are that they are not long-lived, as the chemicals are, and they are not dangerous to humans and most other animal wildlife. Some of them are toxic to fish and should not be used around pools, ponds, streams, creeks, or any area where rain will leach them into bodies of water.

Pyrethrins are made from a species of chrysanthemum. Experience has shown that they work better when an activator such as piperonyl butoxide or piperonyl cyclonene is added. The pyrethrins must make direct contact with the insect to be effective. They will kill aphids, whiteflies, leafhoppers, and thrips. They are ineffective against mites. Since they must make contact, they should be used when the insects are seen. They are dangerous to fish.

Rotenone is made from the derris root, which is ground into a powder. It is also dangerous to fish. Rotenone will kill aphids, spittle bugs, caterpillars, mosquitoes, carpenter ants, chinch bugs, pea weevils, and house flies. It is ineffective against spider mites and soil insects.

Nicotine sulfate, a derivative of tobacco, can be used to kill aphids, whiteflies, leafhopper, thrips, and spider mites. Other botanical insecticides include quassia (made from a Latin American tree), ryania (made from a Latin American shrub), and hellebore (made from lilies).

Biodegradable synthetic insecticides include Sevin, 50 percent of which is gone within three days and 100 percent within two weeks, and malathion, which is completely gone within a week. Both are toxic to fish, but have shown to be nonhazardous to bird and other animal wildlife.

You can also make your own pesticide. Observe which plants are being bothered by a certain pest and which are not. Select a plant, preferably a weed, that is not being bothered by the pest you wish to control. Remove the plant and run it through a meat grinder. Save the liquid and plant residue. Measure what you have and add an equal amount of water. Sprinkle or spray the liquid on the plants you want to protect.

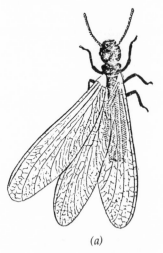
(a)

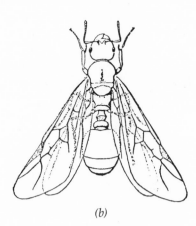
(b)

Fig. 12-5 *a) Termite, b) Ant*

Certain plants are known to repel insects and are a good choice to use near other plants that are bothered by the pests. Nasturtiums are used against aphids and tansy against cutworms and cabbageworms. Rue, marigolds, asters, cosmos, and coreopsis are all known to repel bugs. Garlic, chives, savory, and thyme will spice up your salads and other foods and reduce the number of insects pestering other plants while they are growing.

One of the best ways to eliminate the insect pests is to eliminate those plants pestered by the insects. Keep lists showing which plants are bothered and which are not. Remove those that are constantly being bothered and increase those that are not. By increasing the variety of plants you will have fewer problems. A greater variety of plants attracts a greater variety of pests, providing more food for the pest predators. A greater variety reduces the chance of disaster striking because you have too many plants of the same kind. Variety reduces vulnerability to insect problems.

FERTILIZERS

If you need a fertilizer to keep a plant alive, you are better off letting it die. If you know in advance that you will have to fertilize a plant once you put it in the ground, you should restrain yourself from planting it. This course of action may sound a bit harsh, but think about the process for just a moment. If the plant needs fertilizer to stay alive, it is not very well suited to the soil, climate, and other conditions that exist on your natural landscape. Perhaps the plant would survive better in a different soil, a different part of the country, or a different terrain. You are trying to build a natural environment, not one filled with plants so pampered that they collapse the minute you look the other way. Hardy healthy plants suited for the environment that exists on your property will not need such coddling—especially with chemical fertilizers.

IMPROVING THE SOIL

If chemical fertilizers are needed only when you plant exotic plants, is there need to improve the soil in other ways? The best advice is to take a look around your landscape. Are the plants hardy, healthy, and growing properly? Or are they slowly dying, is their growth stunted, or are they afflicted by so many insect pests that even the birds are having a difficult time keeping the area clean?

If the trees, bushes, shrubs, ground covers, perennials, wildflowers, alpines, and so forth on your natural landscape are hardy and healthy you should be happy. Stop worrying and forget about trying to improve your soil. You have achieved the minimum-maintenance natural landscape.

If your plants are in poor shape, or if you haven't been able to get anything to grow on your land, one of the most likely reasons is that your soil is so poor it won't support life. If your property is so desolate that it resembles a training ground for astronauts, you probably need more help than we can give you here.

Before you do anything to change or improve the nature of your soil, you can have it tested by the local state agricultural extension service. Their report will tell you about the soil's pH, the measurement of its acidity or alkalinity. A pH of 4 is a highly acid soil. A pH of 9 is a highly alkaline soil. A pH of 7 indicates a neutral soil, one that is neither acidic nor alkaline. Adding lime raises the soil's pH. An alkaline soil is treated by adding elemental sulfur, iron sulfate, or aluminum sulfate to lower the soil's pH.

If you have just a few problems with your soil and are unwilling to eliminate troubled plants, a good way to improve the soil and create a natural mulch is composting.

Composts.   A compost heap recycles nature's "wastes" and those from your table into organic healthy food for your plants. It is a handy place to get rid of dead foliage, vegetable tops and peelings, grass clippings, and any other plant material that will rot quickly. Many different compost procedures have been devised and recommended in books and journals. Many different compost structures have been built. One of the easiest is described by the U.S. Department of Agriculture:

> Dig your pit three to four feet deep and as wide and as long as your needs (and waste supply) dictate. Line the sides with boards.

> Put in a six-inch layer of plant material. Sprinkle this layer with lime and 5-10-5 fertilizer—one cup of each to a square yard of litter.

> Add a thin layer of soil to keep the litter in place. Wet down thoroughly.

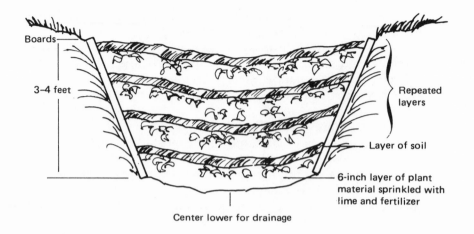

Fig. 12-6 *Compost pit*

Repeat as often as you accumulate enough plant material, until the compost pit is filled.

Make the center lower than the sides, to allow rainfall to drain into the litter. Cover with plastic so the compost will not dry out. Cut a hole one inch in diameter in the center of the plastic so the water will drain into the litter. Water as often as necessary to keep the compost moist.

Turn the pit contents top to bottom after three or four months.

Compost made this way will be ready to use the following spring. At that time, start a second pit. That way you will have one pit with compost ready to use, and one to put to use when you clean up the yard.

You can compost almost any plant material. In addition to those mentioned above, you can also add the following to your compost pit: prunings (unless you have a compost shredder, do not use any woody stems that are thicker than a lead pencil because they don't decompose rapidly enough), sawdust, small wood chips, fireplace ashes, and vacuum cleaner dust. Items that should not be placed on the compost heap include: rags, bones, paper (there is some debate about paper, but the hazards posed by ink preclude putting it on the heap), plastic, grease, paint, oil, and any spiny plant matter that will not break down rapidly.

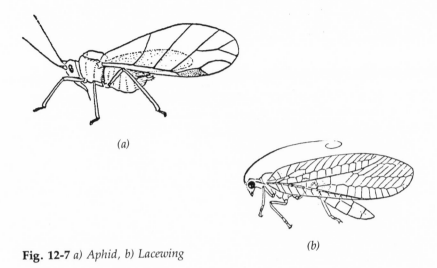

Fig. 12-7 *a) Aphid, b) Lacewing*

Bacterial action heats the compost heap up to between 120° and 160°F. These temperatures are hot enough to kill most weed seeds and plant or animal disease organisms that might be present. So you don't have to worry that, by spreading compost around your plants, you will be adding to the weed population.

Good composting requires air and moisture. One of the reasons for turning the heap is to give those parts that did not decompose access to air and moisture they may have missed. Another way to add air is to take a one-inch pipe and pound it down through the compost heap and then remove it. Do this in several places around the heap and the resulting holes will allow more air into the pile. Be careful to use the right amount of water on the heap. Too much water, soaking the compost pile, prevents air from moving through and a soggy pile will not decompose as rapidly. Too little water and the action of microbes breaking down the plant matter stops. If the compost heap is warm (steamingly so in the winter time) and smells, then you know everything is working as it should.

This compost can be spread one to two inches deep anywhere you think the plants need help. It can also be used as a mulch around plants, although it should be used with caution around perennials since the moisture it will retain may help cause crown rot.

Composting is nature's way of providing plants with extra food. At first it may not seem easier than applying chemical fertilizers, but

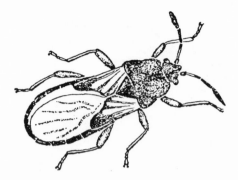

Fig. 12-8 *Chinch bug*

over the long run it is. There are too many mistakes and hazards to contend with in the use of chemical fertilizers. Besides, this way the leaves, grass clippings, and other "wastes" put back into the earth what the plants took out. And it is quite a bit cheaper than purchasing fertilizers, which could be better used to grow food for the world's hungry.

Mulches.   One other tool you can use in your natural landscape to improve the soil is mulching. Any mulch will also save you the time spent cultivating and weeding. If you don't plan to cultivate, don't worry about mulching unless you live in a drought-prone region where mulches help hold soil moisture. An organic mulch has the added benefit of bringing organic matter to the soil as it decomposes and improving the soil's nutritional value for the plants.

Mulches conserve soil water. Moisture is lost from the soil through runoff, transpiration through the plant's leaves, evaporation from the soil's surface, and percolation down through the soil. Mulches reduce loss from runoff by absorbing and holding the water, and from evaporation by forming a protective coating above the soil so that the sun and wind cannot reach the moisture.

Mulches also minimize temperature swings in the soil, reducing freezing and thawing. This is especially valuable in the winter when repeated freezing and thawing will heave plants out of the soil, tearing their roots. Plants subjected to this type of damage will be helped to winter over without heaving by a mulch. Organic mulches tend to insulate soils, but gravels tend to conduct the heat. A dark gravel, for example, will tend to warm up a light-colored soil. An organic mulch will tend to keep the soil cool. These characteristics can be used to speed up or slow down spring growth.

Mulches include straw, hay corncobs, cornstalks, shredded tobacco stems, tanbark, shredded bark and wood, fine bark mulch, coarse bark chips, sawdust (preferably old and partially rotted), wood shavings, shredded leaves, fresh lawn cuttings, compost, coffee grinds, nut shells, peat moss, sugarcane residue, buckwheat hulls, cocoa bean hulls, plastic, aluminum foil, and gravel.

Organic mulches will attract insects, slugs, cutworms, and the birds that eat them. Inorganic mulches don't attract any pests.

The best time to apply a three- to four-inch mulch is in the spring after a long rain has soaked the ground. Wait until after the rain so you won't have to water. Nature will have done it for you. If you are going to apply a winter mulch, wait until the ground has frozen. Any earlier and the mulch will stimulate new growth, which won't have time to harden and will be damaged by the winter freeze.

PREDATORS

Animals can sometimes be most unwelcome in your grounds. They may burrow under the soil, eat the new growth on some of your plants, and make a general nuisance of themselves. Moles and shrews are often attracted to soils rich in organic matter. Daffodils, spurge, and castor bean plants have been found to repel them. Mothballs placed in the mole's burrows will also act as a repellent.

Rabbits love to nibble on vegetable growth, especially new growth. Wire fences usually will make them keep their distance. Since they are vegetarians, blood meal or dried blood will also keep them away. And onions planted among your other plants will repel rabbits.

When questioned about how to get rid of moles, one natural landscape authority said "What harm are they doing? Learn to live with them." So why not sit back and enjoy the rabbits, squirrels, raccoons, deer, woodchucks, and gophers when they come onto your landscape. After all, they are part of what you want to see there—nature.

WHERE 13
TO FIND
FURTHER
HELP

Perhaps you need more information about a plant you are considering. One of your favorite trees may have come down with a disease. You want to have your soil tested. You are fresh out of ideas for a landscape design plan and want to go beyond what you have found here. Where do you turn?

Among the sources for additional information are arboretums, botanical gardens, the U.S. Department of Agriculture, your state agricultural extension service, books and pamphlets listed in the bibliography, local garden clubs, the garden editor of your local newspaper, and landscape architects. Each has a specialty; each is best equipped to help you in his or her area.

Arboretums and botanical gardens are worth visiting to see what they are growing—especially if they are more or less in the same climate and environment as your own. Some are also attached to libraries and can provide reference services. For example, for New Yorkers the Brooklyn Botanic Garden has its own publishing program, which supplies low-cost accurate information.

The U.S. Department of Agriculture issues enough publications to fill a list over 125 pages long. Many are of interest to the natural landscaper, others are meant for the farmer or the home economist. Quite a few of the publications are free; others are for sale. Before you order a document for sale from the Government Printing Office, request it from your senator or representative. They have a quota of books and other documents that ordinarily are for sale, but which they can distribute free. A particularly popular publication may not be available, however.

You don't have to be a VIP to request these services from your elected representatives. Congressmen are used to receiving such re-

Fig. 13-1 *Some of the trees at the Arnold Arboretum outside of Boston (Photo by Dean M. Gottehrer)*

quests from their voters and they will make every effort to meet your request. Your vote counts on election day.

Many of the books and some of the other publications are also available at your local library. Some representatives make it a habit to donate copies of these publications to libraries in their district. Check with the library if you just want to look at a publication and are not interested in owning it.

Your state agricultural extension service is the place to turn to if you want your soil tested. Write for information, forms, and any charges. And you may call the local cooperative extension service office with specific questions about local vegetation, pests, diseases, gardening practices, and so forth. They have access to information and references that can save you research time; if they don't have the information, they may be able to refer you to other sources that do.

Often a local garden club has a wealth of information waiting to be tapped. Its members are people who have worked the soil in your area and can be consulted about specific problems. The garden editor

Fig. 13-2 *Evergreens at Winterthur in Delaware (Photo by Dean M. Gottehrer)*

of your local newspaper is in somewhat the same position. He or she has been covering the activities of gardeners in your area and is likely either to know the answer to your question or to be able to refer you to local residents who do. Don't be afraid to call. Your question may provide the editor with an idea for an article or a column.

Finally, you may decide not to do your own design. Or you may want to consult a professional designer about some aspect of your natural landscape. The professional in this field is the landscape architect. In spite of a trend toward naturalistic landscaping, most landscape architects are schooled to create much more structured designs

Fig. 13-3 *The fountains and conservatory at Longwood Gardens outside of Philadelphia (Photo by Dean M. Gottehrer)*

than those discussed here and may add 10 to 25 percent to the cost of the plant material and installation charges. They do have the advantage of knowing the local climate, the plants that grow successfully in it, and the local suppliers. As with any professional you are going to hire, you need to make a good marriage. Be sure that he or she has done the kind of work for which you are looking. Don't be afraid to ask if you may look at the architect's previous designs and speak with other clients. You are paying for the service and have that right. The architect is an excellent source of information and ought to be able to answer your questions as well as design the particular type of landscape you are looking for for your home. If you aren't satisfied after an initial conversation, look for another landscape architect.

ARBORETUMS, BOTANICAL GARDENS, AND OTHER PLACES OF LANDSCAPE INTEREST

Arnold Arboretum
Jamaica Plain, MA 02130

Fig. 13-4 *A section of the tropical plant display at the Montreal Botanical Garden (Photo by Dean M. Gottehrer)*

Bartlett Arboretum
151 Brookdale Road
Stamford, CT 06903

Bayard Cutting Arboretum
Montauk Highway
Oakdale, Long Island, NY 11769

W.J. Beal Botanical Garden
Michigan State University
East Lansing, MI 48823

Bellingrath Gardens
Theodore, AL 36582

Berkshire Garden Center
Stockbridge, MA 01262

Biltmore House and Gardens
Askeville, NC 28803

Alfred L. Boerner Botanical Gardens
5879 S. 92nd Street
Hales Corner, WI 53130

Botanic Garden Conservatory
1st Street S.W. and Maryland Avenue
Washington, DC 20024

Bowman's Hill Wild Flower Preserve
Washington Crossing, PA 18977

Boyce Thompson Southwest Arboretum
Superior, AZ 85273

Brookgreen Gardens
Murrells Inlet, SC 29576

Brooklyn Botanic Garden
1000 Washington Avenue
Brooklyn, NY 11225

University of California Botanical Garden
Centennial Drive
Berkeley, CA 94720

Callaway Gardens
Route 27
Pine Mountain, GA 31822

Chicago Horticultural Society Botanic Garden
Lake Cook Road
Glencoe, IL 60022

Connecticut Arboretum
Connecticut College
New London, CT 06320

Corkscrew Swamp Sanctuary
Box 1875, Route 6
Sanctuary Road
Naples, FL 33940

The Cornell Plantations
100 Judd Falls Road
Ithaca, NY 14853

Dawes Arboretum
Newark, OH 43055

Denver Botanic Gardens
909 York Street
Denver, CO 80206

Descanso Gardens
1418 Descanso Drive
La Canada, CA 91011

Desert Botanical Garden of Arizona
6400 E. McDowell Road
Phoenix, AZ 85010

Sara P. Duke Memorial Gardens
Duke University
Durham, NC 27706

Fairchild Tropical Garden
10901 Old Cutler Road
Miami, FL 33156

Fernwood, Inc.
1720 Range Line Road
Niles, MI 49120

Forth Worth Botanic Garden
3220 Botanic Garden Drive
Fort Worth, TX 76107

Foster Botanic Garden
50 N. Vineyard Boulevard
Honolulu, HI 96817

Garfield and Lincoln Park Conservatories
Chicago, IL 60600

Hayes Regional Arboretum
801 Elks Road
Richmond, IN 47374

Heritage Plantation
Grove and Pine Streets
Sandwich, MA 02563

Highland and Duran-Eastman Park Arboretum
375 Westfall Road
Rochester, NY 14620

Hodges Gardens
Route 171
Many, LA 71449

Holden Arboretum
Sperry Road
Mentor, OH 44060

Houston Arboretum and Botanical Garden
4501 Woodway
Houston, TX 77024

Hoyt Arboretum
4000 S.W. Fairview Boulevard
Portland, OR 97221

Walter Hunnewell Pinetum
845 Washington Street
Wellesley, MA 02181

Huntington Botanical Gardens
1151 Oxford Road
San Marino, CA 91108

Kingwood Center
Route 430
Mansfield, OH 44906

George Landis Arboretum
Esperance, NY 12066

Living Desert State Park
Carlsbad, NM 88220

Longwood Gardens
Kennett Square, PA 19348

Los Angeles State and County Arboretum
301 North Baldwin Avenue
Arcadia, CA 91006

Magnolia Gardens
Route 4
Charleston, SC 29407

Maimea Arboretum
59-864 Kamehameha Highway
Haleiwa, HI 96712

Matthaei Botanical Gardens
University of Michigan
800 Dixboro Road
Ann Arbor, MI 48105

Memphis Botanic Garden
750 Cherry Road
Memphis, TN 38117

Meyer Arboretum
Ward Pound Ridge Reservation
Cross River, NY 10518

Middleton Place
Route 4
Charleston, SC 29407

University of Minnesota Landscape Arboretum
3675 Arboretum Drive
Chaska, MN 55318

Missouri Botanical Garden
2345 Tower Grove Road
St. Louis, MO 63110

Montreal Botanical Garden
4101 Sherbrooke Street East
Montreal, Canada H1X 2B2

Morris Arboretum
9414 Meadowbrook Avenue
Philadelphia, PA 19118

Morton Arboretum
Lisle, IL 60532

Mount Airy Arboretum
5038 Colerain Avenue
Cincinnati, OH 45223

Mount Auburn Cemetery
580 Mount Auburn Street
Cambridge, MA 02138

Muir Woods National Monument
Mill Valley, CA 94941

National Arboretum
24th and R Streets, N.E.
Washington, DC 20002

New Jersey Agriculture Experiment Station Arboretum
Rutgers University
New Brunswick, NJ 08903

New York Botanical Garden
Bronx Park
New York, NY 10458

Norfolk Botanical Gardens
Airport Road
Norfolk, VA 23518

Old Westbury Gardens
71 Old Westbury Road
Old Westbury, Long Island, NY 11568

Phipps Conservatory
Schenley Park
Pittsburgh, PA 15213

Planting Fields
Oyster Bay, Long Island, NY 11771

Rancho Santa Ana Botanic Garden
1500 N. College Avenue
Claremont, CA 91711

Stanley M. Rowe Arboretum
4500 Muchmore Road
Cincinnati, OH 45243

Santa Barbara Botanic Garden
1212 Mission Canyon Road
Santa Barbara, CA 93105

Arthur Hoyt Scott Horticultural Foundation
Swarthmore College
Swarthmore, PA 19081

Sonnenberg Gardens
151 Charlotte Street
Canandaigua, NY 14424

Strybing Arboretum and Botanic Garden
Golden Gate Park
San Francisco, CA 94122

Tennessee Botanical Gardens and Fine Arts Center
Cheekwood Mansion
Nashville, TN 37205

John J. Tyler Arboretum
515 Painter Road
Lima, PA 19037

University of Washington Arboretum
Lake Washington Boulevard
Seattle, WA 98105

Winterthur
Route 52
Winterthur, DE 19735

University of Wisconsin Arboretum
1207 Seminole Highway
Madison, WI 53711

U.S. DEPARTMENT OF AGRICULTURE

To obtain free publications, write to: Publications Division, Office of Communication, U.S. Department of Agriculture, Washington, DC

20250. On a post card, write your name and address including the zip code. Request no more than ten publications at any one time. List the publications by title and series number. List same series together and in numerical order. To obtain publications for sale, write first to your congressman (see above). If you cannot obtain the publication free, write to: Superintendent of Documents, Government Printing Office, Washington, DC 20402. Prices can be obtained on request. (Publications listed here are not listed in the bibliography.)

Free Publications

Title	Series #
AUTUMN OLIVE FOR WILDLIFE AND OTHER CONSERVATION USES (1972)	L 458
BARK MULCH: NATURAL ARTISTRY AROUND YOUR HOUSE (1975)	L 560
BETTER LAWNS, ESTABLISHMENT, MAINTENANCE, RENOVATION, LAWN PROBLEMS, GRASSES (1971)	G 51
BUILDING A POND (1973)	F 2256
COLOR IT GREEN WITH TREES (1972)	PA 791
CONTROLLING THE TENT CATERPILLAR (1973)	G 178
THE EFFECTS OF SOILS AND FERTILIZERS ON THE NUTRITIONAL QUALITY OF PLANTS (1965)	AB 299
FERN VALLEY TRAIL. THE NATIONAL ARBORETUM (1974)	PA 879
GROWING AZALEAS AND RHODODENDRONS (1975)	G 71
GROWING FLOWERING PERENNIALS (1970)	G 114
GROWING GROUND COVERS (1973)	G 175

Title	Series #
THE GYPSY MOTH AND ITS NATURAL ENEMIES (1975)	AB 381
HOW TO CONTROL WIND EROSION (1972)	AB 354
INVITE BIRDS TO YOUR HOME—CONSERVATION PLANTINGS FOR THE MIDWEST (1971)	PA 982
INVITE BIRDS TO YOUR HOME—CONSERVATION PLANTINGS FOR THE NORTHEAST (1969)	PA 940
KNOW YOUR SOIL (1970)	AB 267
LIST OF AVAILABLE PUBLICATIONS OF THE U.S. DEPARTMENT OF AGRICULTURE	LT 11
MAKING LAND PRODUCE USEFUL WILDLIFE (1969)	F 2035
MORE WILDLIFE THROUGH SOIL AND WATER CONSERVATION (1971)	AB 175
MULCHES FOR YOUR GARDEN (1971)	G 185
POISON IVY, POISON OAK, AND POISON SUMAC: IDENTIFICATION, PRECAUTIONS, ERADICATION (1971)	F 1972

Title	*Series #*
PRUNING ORNAMENTAL SHRUBS AND VINES (1969)	G 165
PRUNING SHADE TREES AND REPAIRING THEIR INJURIES (1965)	G 83
RARE AND LOCAL CONIFERS IN THE UNITED STATES (1975)	CRR 19
RUSSIAN-OLIVE FOR WILDLIFE AND OTHER CONSERVATION USES (1971)	L 517
SAFE USES OF PESTICIDES IN THE HOME—IN THE GARDEN (1972)	PA 589
SELECTING AND GROWING SHADE TREES (1973)	G 205

Title	*Series #*
SELECTING SHRUBS FOR SHADY AREAS (1974)	G 142
SHRUBS, VINES, AND TREES FOR SUMMER COLOR (1972)	G 181
SPRING FLOWERING BULBS (1971)	G 136
SUMMER FLOWERING BULBS (1971)	G 151
TREES OF THE FOREST: THEIR BEAUTY AND USE (1971)	PA 613
THE UNITED STATES NATIONAL ARBORETUM, WASHINGTON, D.C. (1970)	PA 309
WINDBREAKS FOR CONSERVATION (1969)	AB 339

Publications for Sale

Title	*Series #*
ATLAS OF UNITED STATES TREES. VOLUME 1. CONIFERS AND IMPORTANT HARDWOODS	M 1146
ATLAS OF UNITED STATES TREES. VOLUME 2. ALASKA TREES AND COMMON SHRUBS	M 1293
GRASS (YEARBOOK—1948)	YB 1948
INSECTS (YEARBOOK—1952)	YB 1952
LAND (YEARBOOK—1958)	YB 1958
LANDSCAPE FOR LIVING (YEARBOOK—1972)	YB 1972
PLANT DISEASES (YEARBOOK—1953)	YB 1953

Title	*Series #*
PROTECTING SHADE TREES DURING HOME CONSTRUCTION	G 104
SEEDS (YEARBOOK—1961)	YB 1961
SHADE TREES FOR THE HOME (1972)	AH 425
SOIL (YEARBOOK—1957)	YB 1957
TREES (YEARBOOK—1949)	YB 1949
WATER (YEARBOOK—1955)	YB 1955
WILDLIFE FOR TOMORROW (1972)	PA 989
WOOD HANDBOOK (1974)	AH 72

AGRICULTURAL EXTENSION SERVICE OFFICES

Auburn University
Auburn, AL 36830

University of Alaska
College, AK 99735

College of Agriculture
University of Arizona
Tucson, AZ 85721

Division of Agriculture
University of Arkansas
Fayetteville, AR 72701

College of Agriculture
University of California
Berkeley, CA 94720

Colorado State University
Fort Collins, CO 80521

Connecticut Agricultural Experiment Station
New Haven, CT 06504

College of Agriculture
University of Connecticut
Storrs, CT 06268

College of Agricultural Sciences
University of Delaware
Newark, DE 19711

University of Florida
Gainesville, FL 32601

College of Agriculture
University of Georgia
Athens, GA 30602

University of Hawaii
Honolulu, HI 96822

College of Agriculture
University of Idaho
Moscow, ID 83843

College of Agriculture
University of Illinois
Urbana, IL 61801

Purdue University
Lafayette, IN 47907

Iowa State University
Ames, IA 50010

College of Agriculture
Kansas State University
Manhattan, KS 66502

College of Agriculture
University of Kentucky
Lexington, KY 40506

Agricultural College
Louisiana State University
Baton Rouge, LA 70803

College of Agriculture
University of Maine
Orono, ME 04473

University of Maryland
College Park, MD 20742

College of Agriculture
University of Massachusetts
Amherst, MA 01002

College of Agriculture
Michigan State University
East Lansing, MI 48823

College of Agriculture
University of Minnesota
St. Paul, MN 55101

Mississippi State University
State College, MS 39762

College of Agriculture
University of Missouri
Columbia, MO 65201

Montana State University
Bozeman, MT 59715

College of Agriculture
University of Nebraska
Lincoln, NB 68503

College of Agriculture
University of Nevada
Reno, NV 89507

University of New Hampshire
Durham, NH 03824

College of Agriculture
Rutgers University
New Brunswick, NJ 08903

College of Agriculture
New Mexico State University
University Park, NM 88071

College of Agriculture
Cornell University
Ithaca, NY 14850

College of Agriculture
North Carolina State University
Raleigh, NC 27602

North Dakota State University
Fargo, ND 58102

College of Agriculture
Ohio State University
Columbus, OH 43210

Oklahoma State University
Stillwater, OK 74074

Oregon State University
Corvallis, OR 97331

Pennsylvania State University
University Park, PA 16802

University of Puerto Rico
Rio Piedras, PR 00928

University of Rhode Island
Kingston, RI 02881

Clemson University
Clemson, SC 29631

South Dakota State University
Brookings, SD 57006

College of Agriculture
University of Tennessee
Knoxville, TN 37916

Texas A & M University
College Station, TX 77843

College of Agriculture
Utah State University
Logan, UT 84321

State Agricultural College
University of Vermont
Burlington, VT 05401

Virginia Polytechnic Institute
Blacksburg, VA 24061

Washington State University
Pullman, WA 99163

West Virginia University
Morgantown, WV 26506

College of Agriculture
University of Wisconsin
Madison, WI 53706

College of Agriculture
University of Wyoming
Laramie, WY 83071

Federal Extension Service
U.S. Department of Agriculture
Washington, DC 20250

BIBLIOGRAPHY

Publications listed under the U.S. Department of Agriculture are not included here.

Aiken, George D., *Pioneering with Wildflowers*, Prentice-Hall, 1968.

Billard, Ruth Sawyer, *Birdscaping Your Yard*, State of Connecticut, Department of Environmental Protection, 1972.

Birdseye, Clarence and Eleanor, *Growing Woodland Plants*, Dover Publications, 1951.

Bloom, Alan, *Perennials for Your Garden*, Charles Scribner's Sons, 1974.

Brainerd, John, *Working with Nature*, Oxford University Press, 1973.

Brimer, John B., *The Home Gardener's Guide to Trees and Shrubs*, Hawthorn, 1976.

Brooklyn Botanic Garden Handbooks (available for $1.75 each postage paid from Brooklyn Botanic Garden, 1000 Washington Avenue, Brooklyn, NY 11225).

    10. Rock Gardens
    14. Vines
    20. Soils
    22. Broad-leaved Evergreens
    23. Mulches
    25. 100 Finest Trees and Shrubs
    31. Bulbs
    34. Biological Control of Plant Pests
    38. Gardening with Wildflowers
    41. Flowering Trees
    44. Flowering Shrubs
    50. Garden Pests
    63. 1200 Trees and Shrubs—Where to Buy Them
    65. Tree and Shrub Forms—Their Landscape Use
    66. Rhododendrons and Their Relatives
    71. The Home Lawn Handbook
    73. Weed Control
    77. Natural Gardening

Bruce, Hal, *How to Grow Wildflowers and Wild Shrubs and Trees*, Knopf, 1976.

Bruning, Walter F., *Minimum Maintenance Gardening Handbook*, Harper & Row, 1971.

Campbell, Stu, *Let It Rot! The Home Gardener's Guide to Composting*, Garden Way Publishing, 1975.

Campbell, Stu, *The Mulch Book*, Garden Way Publishing, 1974.

Crockett, James Underwood, *Landscape Gardening*, Time-Life Books, 1971.

Dana, Mrs. William Starr, *How to Know the Wild Flowers*, Dover Publications.

Davison, Verne E., *Attracting Birds from the Prairies to the Atlantic*, T. Y. Crowell Co., 1967.

Dennis, John V., *A Complete Guide to Bird Feeding*, Knopf, 1975.

Eaton, Leonard K., *Landscape Artist in America: The Life and Work of Jens Jensen*, University of Chicago Press, 1964.

Eckbo, Garrett, *The Art of Home Landscaping*, F. W. Dodge Corporation, 1956.

Eckbo, Garrett, *Landscape for Living*, F.W. Dodge Corporation, 1950.

Editors of *Organic Gardening*, *Lawn Beauty the Organic Way*, Rodale Books, 1970.

Encyclopedia of Organic Gardening, Rodale Books, 1969.

Flemer, William, *Nature's Guide to Successful Gardening and Landscaping*, T.Y. Crowell Co., 1972.

Foley, Daniel J., *Ground Covers for Easier Gardening*, Dover Publications, 1961.

Foster, H. Lincoln, *Rock Gardening*, Bonanza Books, 1968.

Grimm, William C., *Recognizing Native Shrubs*, Stackpole Books, 1966.

Heritage, Bill, *The Lotus Book of Water Gardening*, Hamlyn, London, 1973.

Hersey, Jean, *Wild Flowers to Know and Grow*, Van Nostrand, 1964.

Hotchkiss, Neil, *Common Marsh, Underwater and Floating-leaved Plants of the United States and Canada*, Dover Publications, 1972.

Howard, Francis, *Landscaping with Vines*, Macmillan, 1959.

Hunter, Beatrice Trim, *Gardening Without Poisons*, Houghton Mifflin, 1964.

Ireys, Alice, *How to Plan and Plant Your Own Property*, Morrow, 1975.

Jensen, Jens, *Siftings*, Ralph Fletcher Seymour, 1939.

Keeler, Harriet, *Our Northern Shrubs*, Dover Publications, 1969.

Kenfield, Warren G., *The Wild Gardener in The Wild Landscape: The Art of Naturalistic Landscaping*, Hafner Publishing Co., 1966.

Kilvert, B. Cory, Jr., *Informal Gardening*, Macmillan, 1969.

Kolaga, Walter A., *All About Rock Gardens and Plants*, Doubleday, 1966.

Kramer, Jack, *The Natural Way to Pest-Free Gardening*, Charles Scribner's Sons, 1972.

Kramer, Jack, *Water Gardening*, Charles Scribner's Sons, 1971.

Martin, Alexander C. with Herbert S. Zim and Arnold L. Nelson, *American Wildlife & Plants: A Guide to Wildlife Food Habits*, Dover Publications, 1951.

McElroy, Thomas P., Jr., *The Habitat Guide to Birding*, Knopf, 1974.

McElroy, Thomas P., Jr., *The New Handbook of Attracting Birds*, Knopf, 1960.

National Wildlife Federation, *Gardening With Wildlife*, 1974.

Nehrling, Arno and Irene, *Easy Gardening with Drought-Resistant Plants*, Dover Publications, 1968.

Niering, William A. with Richard H. Goodwin, *Creating New Landscapes With Herbicides: A Homeowner's Guide*, Connecticut Arboretum, 1963.

Niering, William A. with Richard H. Goodwin, *Energy Conservation on the Home Grounds: The Role of Naturalistic Landscaping*, Connecticut Arboretum, July 1975.

Organic Way to Plant Protection, Rodale Books, 1966.

Ortloff, H. Stuart and Henry B. Raymore, *The Book of Landscape Design*, M. Barrows & Company, 1959.

Peterson, Roger Tory and Margaret McKenny, *A Field Guide to Wildflowers*, Houghton Mifflin, 1968.

Philbrick, Helen and Richard Gregg, *Companion Plants and How to Use Them*, Devin, 1966.

Philbrick, John and Helen, *The Bug Book: Harmless Insect Controls*, Garden Way Publishing, 1974.

Rickett, Harold William, *Wild Flowers of the United States*, McGraw-Hill, 1966.

Riker, Tom with Harvey Rottenberg, *The Gardener's Catalogue*, Morrow, 1974.

Robinson, W., *Alpine Flowers for Gardens*, John Murray, London, 1903.

Rock Gardens and Pools, Castle Books, 1974.

Rodale, J. I., and staff, *How to Landscape Your Own Home*, Rodale Books, 1963.

Sears, Paul Bigelow with Marion Rombauer and Francis Jones Poetker, *Wild Wealth*, Bobbs-Merrill, 1971.

Schuler, Stanley, *Make Your Garden New Again*, Simon and Shuster, 1975.

Shewell-Cooper, W.E., *The Basic Book of Rock Gardens and Pools*, Drake Publishers, 1973.

Steffek, Edwin F., *Wildflowers and How to Grow Them*, Crown, 1953.

Taylor, Kathryn and Stephen F. Hamblin, *Handbook of Wildflower Cultivation*, Macmillan, 1963.

Taylor, Norman, *The Guide to Garden Shrubs and Trees*, Houghton Mifflin, 1965.

Taylor, Norman, *Taylor's Encyclopedia of Gardening*, Houghton Mifflin, 1961.

Thomas, Dr. G.L., Jr., *Garden Pools, Water-Lilies, and Goldfish*, Van Nostrand, 1958.

Vosburgh, John, *Living with Your Land*, Charles Scribner's Sons, 1968.

Westcott, Cynthia, *The Gardener's Bug Book*, Doubleday, 1973.

Westcott, Cynthia, *Plant Disease Handbook*, Van Nostrand Reinhold, 1971.

Wilder, Louise Beebe, *Hardy Bulbs*, Dover Publications, 1974.

Wilder, Louise Beebe, *The Fragrant Garden*, Dover Publications, 1932.

Wyman, Donald, *Ground Cover Plants*, Macmillan, 1976.

Wyman, Donald, *Shrubs and Vines for American Gardens*, Macmillan, 1969.

Wyman, Donald, *Trees for American Gardens*, Macmillan, 1965.

Wyman, Donald, *Wyman's Gardening Encyclopedia*, Macmillan, 1971.